A Gui

Positive Re

PAID

WITHDRAWN
FROM CROYDON
LIBRARIES

GW00493296

408

2 0 JAN 1995

A Guide to
Positive Retirement

DR PATRICIA GILBERT
MB BS MRCS LRCP DRCOG

GRAFTON BOOKS
A Division of the Collins Publishing Group

LONDON GLASGOW
TORONTO SYDNEY AUCKLAND

Grafton Books
A Division of the Collins Publishing Group
8 Grafton Street, London W1X 3LA

Published by Grafton Books 1988

British Library Cataloguing in Publication Data
Gilbert, Patricia
A guide to positive retirement.
1. Retirement
I. Title
646.7'9   HQ1062

ISBN 0 246 13018 0

Photoset by Rowland Phototypesetting Ltd,
Bury St Edmunds, Suffolk
Printed and Bound in Great Britain by
Hartnolls Limited, Bodmin, Cornwall.

Contents

Introduction

Retirement these days conjures up a very different picture in people's minds from that of even a generation ago. Our parents – and even more so our grandparents – retired from the work by which they earned their daily bread with a sense of relief. They were tired. Physically and mentally they had had enough. Before them lay the prospect of pipe and slippers in the winter and a chair in the sun in the summer. The time had come for them to relax and move gently and imperceptibly downhill into old age.

Attitudes nowadays have moved a good way from that. Go to a retirement party today, and you will be hard pushed to pick out the person for whom the celebration has been arranged: he will by no means be a tired greybeard. And this, of course, also applies to women in retirement. (A colleague of mine retired recently, at the statutory age, and the following week took her first plunge into matrimony. Life had certainly, for her, taken on a completely new dimension.) Retirement from one's main occupation is now often simply a change of direction. New prospects and tasks open up, and many a new career has started a few months after a retirement celebration.

There are many factors at work in producing this change. Earlier retirement can often be taken by, or can indeed be forced upon, both men and women. 'Redundancy' or 'reorganisation' may be the terms under which a job is no longer available. But for you, if this happens, the following Monday morning will hold the same prospects as if you had retired on more conventional terms. Add better health prospects (and hence extra years of life) to this younger retirement age, and retirement can take on a new, exciting character if viewed in the right light. But retirement can also appear daunting. What will there be to do once the relief of not having to catch the 8.15 a.m. train has worn off? Will the companionship of workmates be missed? Will our opinions be thought no longer worth seeking? These and many other questions will cross the minds of those taking early, or enforced, retirement.

This book aims to take a look at some of the more important aspects of these possible problems. Health and fitness are given a major share of attention. With fitness and an active mind many potential pitfalls can be avoided or, if not avoided, overcome. Problems such as housing and finance can have a marked effect on both mental and physical health, and these are also discussed. It is hoped that there will be much to be found in these pages to help you in planning for a happy, productive retirement.

1 · Accepting the challenge

Every phase of life has its advantages and disadvantages and the middle years are no exception. Take a step back from your life for a moment and review the *advantages* of those middle years.

• Gone, to a large extent, are those youthful worries about everyday situations. No longer does the thought of walking into a roomful of strangers cause that thudding heart, blurring of vision and a certain jelly-like wobbling of the knees. No longer does blind panic intervene if a train connection is missed or the traffic queue is seen winding into the far distance. From the more relaxed viewpoint of middle age, we are aware that these problems have arisen before – and what follows is well known. For example, many of those unfamiliar faces will turn out to be friendly, ordinary mortals like ourselves; and chances are high that the other members of the meeting to which we are travelling are also caught in the same traffic snarl-up.

• By the time middle age is reached, views on wider aspects of life are usually well established. No longer do the 'winds of change' blow us from one extreme to the other. Maturity brings the ability to look objectively at new thoughts, ideas and situations, to weigh them up in the light of previous experience and to judge accordingly. The well-adjusted middle-ager (and are we not all 'well-adjusted'?) will be aware of the dangers of harking back to the 'good old days', and will balance views accordingly. The ability to counter the wilder enthusiasms of youth (admittedly a vitally important contribution to many situations) with objective reasoning and sound common sense built on experience is one of the greatest benefits middle-agers can bring to a situation.

• By middle age many everyday lessons of life have been learned.

No longer is the cry 'But it's not fair!' the response when problems arise. As middle age is reached, everyone *knows* that life is not fair – and never will be. So instead of wasting time and energy in kicking against the situation, the middle-ager sets to and tries to resolve the problem in the best way possible.

• Most of the financial crises of youth are now a memory. (Perhaps they are being re-lived at second hand by watching the struggles of the up-and-coming generation, but no longer do they seem such an impenetrable jungle in the light of experience.) Enforced retirement may indeed lead to financial worries and these cannot be dismissed lightly; but experience has taught that by adjusting lifestyle or changing financial direction, for example, the problems are not insurmountable. It is always a good thought that by the time middle age is reached, children are either completely self-supporting, or there are at least signs that they will become so in the not too distant future. There are obvious exceptions to this, of course, particularly in the light of today's employment prospects. But with frank discussion, most families will be able to arrive at some compromise.

Perhaps the *disadvantages* of middle life spring to your mind with greater ease?

• Gone are the days when talking, dancing, eating and drinking until the early hours can be indulged in with impunity. Eating late – and perhaps unwisely – can often lead to that fuller-than-full feeling so beloved of television advertisements. And somehow the tasks of the following day seem extra burdensome after a night out. So a little adjustment of pleasures is necessary. They need by no means be less enjoyable – simply different.

• There has probably never been a generation before the one to which today's middle-agers belong that has seen such dramatic technological advances. And they are still happening, particularly in all methods of communication. For example, video telephones will doubtless soon be commonplace, and electronic money is hovering on the horizon. These and many other aspects of living, which are taken easily into the stride of youth, become harder to grasp and use in the later middle years.

● Unless you are extraordinarily athletic, or have kept yourself relentlessly in trim over the years, your physical powers will not be as great as they were 20 or 30 years ago. Watch a teenager disco-dancing (and remember how *you*, too, danced the twist). If you tried to do it with the same vigour you would at best find it impossible, at worst, you would end up with aching muscles, strained ligaments or broken limbs. So again, activities must be chosen to suit your maturing abilities.

● Then, looks. This aspect is probably of greater importance to women – although men are not immune to resenting a developing paunch and receding hair-line. Skin inevitably becomes drier with the ageing process. Wrinkles appear around eyes and mouth, and those ubiquitous brown patches on the backs of hands seem to appear overnight. Hair greys and also becomes drier and more difficult to manage. Again – do not despair. Wrinkles can be considered as character lines – think of the many pictures and photographs of serene older folk who would not look half as beautiful – yes, beautiful – without their wrinkles. But be determined that *your* wrinkles will be made up of laughter lines and not down-in-the-mouth miserable ones. A little extra attention to your skin daily, and a suitable hair style for ladies will ensure that your looks – although different – will certainly not deteriorate as you get older.

Surprised by the way things seem to be shaping up when you pause to consider, briefly, the advantages and disadvantages of those middle years? Perhaps you can think of more on both sides of the coin?

Before going on to look at some of the ways of ensuring a positive retirement as they may apply to you, let us look at some of the facts that apply generally to people approaching this point.

● In the West there is an ageing population. In Britain in 1951, there were 6.9 million people of retirement age (men of 65 and women of 60) out of a population of 50.5 million. In 1981 – 30 short years later – while the population had risen to 56.3 million, the number of retired people was almost half as much again, at around 10 million.

At first sight this may seem a gloomy picture, but do remember that where there is a need (in this case the needs of the older generation) there will – eventually – be the facilities available to meet it. Both politicians and health services are well aware of the trends in the age of our population. This knowledge, together with pressure and help from such voluntary agencies as Age Concern, are resulting in thought being given to the needs of this important part of the population. Sheltered housing schemes and retirement homes, for example, are becoming a priority in many parts of the country.

● For the vast majority of people, the retirement years will mean 15 to 20 years of active life. The average life expectancy today of women is 78 years, and of men 72 years – a sharp contrast to the expectancy of a century ago. Well known 'long-livers' there were indeed, but they were the exception rather than the rule. Retirement could represent a quarter of your whole life-span, and there is no point in wasting this precious span of years given to us. A little sensible forward planning can do much to make these the best years ever. Suitable living accommodation (and remember that over 95 per cent of over-65s are living in their own homes), sensible eating and a possible rearrangement of your financial plans, together with a little thought into ways of keeping your mind and body in the best possible trim, are all matters you should consider.

● Older people enjoy better health than did their ancestors. Many of the infectious diseases such as tuberculosis, for example, have in the main been conquered. Occupational diseases such as asbestosis (affecting the lungs of workers in the asbestos industry) have been thoroughly researched. A wide range of jobs with occupational hazards are made safe nowadays by a variety of techniques. As a simple example, the wearing of ear-muffs to reduce the sound levels of working conditions such as pneumatic drilling and tractor driving has done much to reduce the incidence of deafness occurring in later life. 'Health and safety' at work has made a very positive impact on everyday living.

● In 1986 there were 136 Members of Parliament out of a total of 650 who were over 60 years of age, and this included the Prime Minister. Again in 1986, there were almost 500 applicants for Open University degrees who were over 65 years of age. All these men and women were certainly not letting their latter years be wasted away.

● Many more retired couples are having to adjust to situations in which:
   a) they still have elderly parents alive;
   b) they may still have responsibility for teenage children.
All three generations may be living under one roof. This will obviously have far-reaching financial and housing implications. Emotional relationships and contrasting lifestyles are also potentially explosive in these circumstances. Again, a clear-headed review (and re-review as the situation alters – as it inevitably will) of possible courses of action will do much to make the best of these potentially trying conditions. As you plan, remember that you too – caught in the middle generation – have needs as well as the younger and older family members.

● For many couples today retirement is not taking place with the partner of the first marriage: in not a few cases, the 'honeymoon' period of the second marriage is hardly over before the changes due to retirement are upon you. Add to this the potential problem of stepchildren who may be in the stormy years of adolescence, and the scene is set for a good deal of stress. This, too, will need to be recognised and adjustments made in lifestyle and maybe also attitudes.

Consideration of all these facts can give you guidelines as to the ways in which your thoughts must be going as you plan your retirement years. But these are generalisations only. No two individual circumstances are the same. As an example, two broad outlines of retirement patterns highlight this difference – perhaps stereotyped, but many people will recognise their life pattern as a variation on the theme.

● The situation where *the wife has either remained at home or has herself retired from outside work, and the husband retires, perhaps prematurely.*

Problems that could arise

A. *from wife's viewpoint*
  1. husband is 'under her feet' all day long;
  2. husband tries to organise her life/kitchen/routine;
  3. she has to think of food at midday;
  4. she has less 'private' time to follow her own interests.

B. *from husband's point of view:*
  1. perhaps little to do, once initial tasks around house are completed;
  2. wife seems to have interests which do not include him;
  3. feelings of being an intruder in his own home.

Possible remedies
  1. Talk about the problems. (This is probably the most important factor in any successful retirement.) Discuss ways in which previous routines can be adjusted to a mutually agreeable pattern.
  2. Try to work out ways in which to do the necessary routine

tasks alongside one another. For example, husband sees to green-house/car/garden while wife does necessary housework/cooking. But do remember the importance of:

3. Having some 'private times', for both partners, when hobbies and other interests can be pursued separately.

4. Wife may need to lower her standards of housework – a layer of dust is far preferable to a widening rift between husband and wife.

5. Husband should remember that his wife has been success-fully coping with the household routine for many years on her own.

6. Above all – and this applies to whatever situation you find yourself in – keep a sense of humour. Laugh *together* at the inevitable misunderstandings and differences of opinion. You know one another a good deal better than when you first got married, but over the years, large periods of daily/weekly/monthly time have been spent apart. Now you must start getting to know each other again under a different set of circumstances.

• This very situation happened to Bob and Madge. Bob had been in teaching all his life. When the opportunity came for early retirement from the headship of a large comprehensive school, after much thought he accepted. All went well for the first few weeks: life seemed just like an extended holiday. But when Bob started taking down the cupboards in the kitchen one day when Madge was out at her dressmaking class, problems began.

'I thought you would prefer to have these cupboards over here, Madge – much easier to work with.' Madge told Bob in no uncertain terms exactly what she thought of his idea. 'I've lived and worked with those cupboards for a good many years now,' was just one of the more polite comments that she made.

Over the next few weeks Bob was quiet, and at times sunk deep in thought. One day, as they were walking in the lanes near their home, he asked Madge how she would feel about the idea of him taking on a part-time post as a specialist teacher to handicapped children. 'I know I have only just retired from teaching, but this would only be very part-time,' he said hesitantly.

To his surprise, Madge welcomed the idea enthusiastically. They would both have their own outside interests, Bob would no longer feel at a loose end all day and their evenings would be interestingly spent in discussing the day's events. But the greatest benefit to Madge, of course, would be that her kitchen would remain exactly as it had always been.

● The situation where *the husband has retired and the wife is still out at full-time work* (and this may well become increasingly common).

Problems that could arise

A. *from wife's viewpoint:*
  1. resentment at husband's relative amount of leisure time;
  2. husband's interference in/incompetence at domestic tasks.

B. *from husband's viewpoint:*
  1. feelings of uselessness;
  2. resentment at role of breadwinner being denied him.

Possible remedies
  1. A specific 'sit-down' review of domestic arrangements, with clear-cut lines of responsibility for specific tasks.
  2. Perhaps an alteration in the standard of house care that is expected.
  3. A definite time – perhaps once a week – when you do something *together* that you both enjoy, be it a visit to the local pub, a meal with friends or the pursuit of a common interest.

The latter situation will probably be the one felt most keenly by men of this present generation. Masculine and feminine roles for these couples have been fairly rigidly stereotyped throughout life. The next generation, with its greater emphasis on husbands and fathers taking a greater part in the day-to-day care of home and children, may well be better adjusted to this increasingly common retirement pattern.

Both these possible patterns of retirement assume a husband/ wife relationship, but there are many people, both men and women, facing retirement on their own. They may be single, divorced or widowed, but whatever the reason, retirement for them will also be a time of change and readjustment. Some more specific problems that can be highlighted under these circumstances are:

Loneliness
Here the retiring person who has always lived alone will be at an advantage over the person who has lost a partner – whether by death, divorce or separation. For the single person, it is only the adjustment to empty – perhaps long – days that will have to be made at retirement. His or her weekends, evenings and other free time will have been already catered for as a single person: such people will be used to organising their own activities and joining groups and discussions on their own. Nevertheless, retirement can still be difficult, especially if friends and contemporaries are still at work during the day. The temptation is great indeed to telephone or visit a friend who has just arrived home from work with suggestions as to how to spend the evening. After a month or two of retirement it can be hard to remember those feelings of exhaustion on returning home from a long day at work. A nearby chair into which to collapse and recoup one's energies is all that is needed before even thinking about the evening's activities. So wait an hour or two before making contact, otherwise a previously flourishing friendship may show signs of wilting.

Try to fill the days usefully and happily with an extension of interests which previously had to be fitted into spare time. Household chores can be spread so that a little is done each day instead of the 'crash' onslaught so often necessary when work takes up a high proportion of time.

For people whose partner has recently died – and especially so if this has occurred just a few months before retirement – loneliness can be a potent factor in the way decisions regarding housing and lifestyle are ultimately made, as the following example shows.

● Jane and Bill had been looking forward eagerly to Bill's retirement. Jane had given up her dressmaking business in anticipation of the extra time they would have to spend together – travelling, visiting the family and pursuing Bill's hobby of photographing exotic birds and flowers. Sadly, Bill suffered a heart attack just six months before his retirement. Two days of agonising worry and distress, while Bill lay fighting for his life in the intensive care unit of the local hospital, had to be endured by Jane before her beloved husband died. Her world – and her plans – had collapsed around her. Friends and family did everything possible to help in the succeeding months. But decisions about the rest of her life – without Bill – had to be made by Jane alone.

Following a three-week visit to her daughter – many miles away – Jane started seriously to consider her future. Should she move to be near her daughter, as she had been pressed to do during the previous weeks? Helen was trying to do a part-time typing course in between looking after her energetic three-year-old daughter and her shift-working husband, and Jane had felt really fulfilled again helping out in this situation.

'But supposing they move?' she mused. 'And is it a good thing to be so involved with the family?' After many wakeful nights thinking about this option, Jane finally decided to stay where she was – at least for the foreseeable future. After all, she had many friends locally, and she was beginning to get involved with local activities again as well as resurrecting some of her old dressmaking contacts. All this would be lost if she moved away from her present home. An old and valued friend had said to her soon after Bill's death, 'Don't move *anywhere* for at least a year, Jane – you'll only regret it.'

Looking back, a couple of years later, Jane realised that she had made the right decision. Whilst life would never be the same without Bill, it still had much to offer. Her days were filled with activity and she looked forward with much pleasure to her twice-yearly visits to her family, who had indeed moved – and not just to another town or country, but to another continent.

'I would have been very lonely now if I had moved two years ago,' she thought, as she hurried to get ready for yet another meeting of the local music society.

This anecdote emphasises the need to think very carefully about any major move in the early stages of any stressful situation. (Remember, too, that retirement itself is a stressful event. In any stress scoring system a change of job is rated fairly high, and what else is retirement but a change of job?)

Running away from loneliness is quite the wrong course of action. You will not want to be working even harder than before retirement, simply to avoid being lonely; but conversely, neither should hobbies, social activities or voluntary work be shelved just because you have reached an age when it is customary to take things a little easier.

Financial pressures.
A pension for a single person, state or occupational, will not stretch as far as a pension for a married couple. Housing and heating costs (two of the largest items in any budget) are the same whether one, two or more people live under one roof.

Divorced and separated women in particular can be under great financial pressure at retirement age. There may well have been long periods of time when the wife was at home looking after the children, or paying only a reduced National Insurance contribution in a part-time job, so at retirement her National Insurance contributions will not be sufficient to earn her a full pension. For divorced women, the government have a concessionary scheme whereby credits can be received on the ex-husband's contributions, if his contribution record is the better of the two. Separated women, however, cannot claim this concession as they are still regarded as their husband's dependant: they will only receive 60 per cent of the full pension.

Help was given to women in these circumstances in 1978 by credits being allowed for 'home responsibility' for women at home looking after children. But there are many women now at retirement age who have not benefited long enough from this piece of legislation for it to make any difference to the pension they will receive at retirement age. The only way to increase income under these circumstances is to apply for supplementary benefit.

For further information on these aspects consult the DHSS leaflet N132A entitled 'Retirement pension if you are divorced or widowed'.

Obviously, finances will have to be carefully assessed and lifestyle adjusted to meet differing needs. Retirement is not something that 'just happens', or at least it should not be. In the same way as you have done throughout life, you should be prepared to work at and 'manage' your retirement. This means not prolonging the holiday spirit for *too* long after you retire, so that you find yourself getting bored with life. It is, of course, good to have an initial period of relaxation after a lifetime of routine – and perhaps stressful – work. But set yourself a definite date – maybe a month or so after your retirement date – when you will start once again to organise the day's activities, although with a far different emphasis from your previous routine.

Many people still find it helpful to keep a diary listing, on the one hand, social and family events and, on the other, tasks that need to be done. A sample couple's diary, for example, could read as follows:

MONDAY	Clean greenhouse	Sow seeds
TUESDAY	Mow grass	Take Aunt Jane to tea
WEDNESDAY	Car for service	Phone Jeff
THURSDAY	Weekly shop	Attend parish meeting
FRIDAY	Round of golf with Bert	

SATURDAY		Local amateur dramatics
SUNDAY	Church	Twins' birthday party

Obviously there will be as many variations on this theme as there are individuals. But writing down events and activities will give a purpose to the day, and a sense of fulfilment at the end of the day. No need to fill the diary completely with activities – leave time for the inevitable chat over the garden fence and the routine chores that need to be done. Holidays, or at least a change of scene, need to come into your management calculations too. Even if these cannot be as exotic or as expensive as those to which you may have been accustomed, it is important that you should have a break in routine – yet another facet of managing your time successfully.

Do not over-manage your schedule, however. Leave time to enjoy your retirement years. It is good to be able to 'stand and stare' – and what better time to do this than when you are retired? Whatever your circumstances, retirement will offer a challenge to you. Remember that ageing does not *start* when you retire, it begins as soon as we stop growing and developing – at about 18 to 20 years of age. So retirement is *not* synonymous with ageing – just a variation in the way we order our lives.

2 · Housing

Retirement, at whatever age, is a good time to review your housing needs. At each time of life housing requirements differ. The young couple with one child will be able to manage quite successfully in the small house or flat in which they started out together, but it is a different picture when perhaps two or three school-age children are trying to fit into the same living area. Then, later, teenagers with friends galore and often weird and wonderful hobbies need space – and parents also need a quiet room or two to themselves. At the time of retirement needs will again be different. Financial considerations are of course closely linked at this phase of life with housing possibilities but, leaving this latter facet aside for the moment, ask yourself a few basic questions as to what is really necessary by way of living accommodation.

Is your house too big? This will, of course, depend on your family circumstances. Several patterns emerge.

1. You will have a number of young people around who still need to be housed (especially likely if you have had to take early retirement for one reason or another). Maybe you have sons or daughters away at university or college who have, as yet, no home of their own. In these circumstances there are two options open to you:

a) Remain in your present home for a further year or two, until your young have finally 'flown the nest' to set up home on their own.

b) Move to a smaller property, that will be eminently suitable for the two of you, and be prepared for chaos in the weeks when the children are at home.

● Ray and Betty lived in a large town house in a provincial city for some time after their return from many years in Africa. They and their children Mark and Penny were happy there. Schools, work, shops and many other facilities were close by and convenient. But within seven years, Mark had gone off to university and Penny had just obtained a place at medical school. For a large part of the year Ray and Betty spread themselves in the space available. The house came to life again in vacations, and was often filled to capacity with the friends of the young people.

After a couple of years, the visits of the young people grew more fleeting – invitations to exotic shores and lively youthful holidays took over. Ray had the opportunity to move to a smaller town on a short-term contract (he was 55 and thought that after this he would be able to take early retirement.) After much discussion, the couple moved to a small village near Ray's work. The bungalow they spent much joyful labour renovating was just what they had always wanted. Mark and Penny were quite delighted to see their parents so settled and happy. They managed to get 'home' as often as before, but extra patience and time spent organising rooms and meals were necessary. As Betty remarked, 'It's lovely to see them, but, oh, so peaceful when they go!'

And all four of the family knew that within a further year or two, both Mark and Penny would be inviting their parents to visit them in their own homes.

2. With early retirement on the cards for many people, it is quite likely that elderly parents will still be alive – maybe both parents, perhaps just one. It is in the latter case, especially when this (perhaps lonely) parent becomes unable to cope adequately alone, that housing needs may have to be re-thought.

Is it wise to take on the perhaps difficult commitment of having a mother or father to live with you? Perhaps a 'granny flat' built on to the house is the answer? Or maybe a move for both of you to separate houses in the same street or village would be a better idea?

The problem is increasing as both men and women are tending to live into advanced old age: in many cases their children are pensioners themselves. Old people's homes are still at a premium, and it is not always the wish of either the elderly parents or their sons and daughters that this should be the answer to the problem of caring adequately for themselves.

Success stories have been reported where all three generations live happily together in one large house, and this may be the answer for you. But do be businesslike about it. Discuss to whom the house will belong – in the joint names of all three of you (husband, wife and mother- or father-in-law) or only in the husband's and wife's names? (Discussion with someone well-versed in the financial implications is important here.) Continue your businesslike thinking into day-to-day living. Each section of the family *must* have a part of the house into which they can retire to be completely by themselves. Have a code that everyone respects, from the eldest member down to the youngest. For example, when Granny feels like a little quiet, she will shut the door into her living quarters. Everyone should then respect her privacy, and only interrupt her in an emergency. This arrangement has much to recommend it if a good, honest relationship exists between elderly parents and children. A final, vital ingredient, also, is the will to make the arrangement work.

3. If it is only husband and wife that have to be considered at retirement age, the situation is again different. They have only themselves to consider. Sounds easy? But it is vital that both partners are in the same mind when it comes to the question of whether or not to move house, especially if this involves a move to a different part of the country – or even a move abroad. Much unhappiness can result if one partner feels that he or she has been forced to move unwillingly. Talk it out thoroughly, looking at both sides of every question. There will doubtless be many facets that will need to be discussed, including that vital one – can you afford to move? It is not much use spending most of your budget on the new building and ending up with curtains/carpets/furniture that fitted admirably into your old house but which do not fit at all into the new property, and finding you have not sufficient money with which to buy new.

Take time over your decision. Remember that there is no need
to hurry now that you have retired.

4. Single people – whether widowed, divorced or unmarried –
have perhaps the most difficult task of all. Not for them the long
intimate discussions with the family about future living accommodation. Friends may be able to give much sensible advice, but
they are not personally involved in decision-making. And interest
will soon flag – especially if a move some distance away is being
contemplated.

Situations vary markedly for such folk. Maybe an unmarried
daughter who has cared for elderly parents all her working life now
finds that she is alone with an enormous family house on her
hands. Or again, a widower has worked for years in a job where his
house was part of his wages. When retirement age comes, not only
is his job finished, but also the roof over his head will disappear.

• Remember not to fall into the trap that closed on Jenny B. She
had recently emerged from a particularly distressing divorce, and
felt the need for a complete change. At 56, she considered herself
lucky to obtain a post as a receptionist/bookkeeper at a large hotel
on a holiday island. Even better, with the job went a neat little
flatlet complete with every possible up-to-date gadget. Following
the divorce, money had been a problem and, after division of the
family home, the type of property Jenny would have been able to
buy was limited in the extreme.

So, despite protestations from friends, Jenny moved into her
new flatlet. She felt a little lonely at first, but soon got into the
swing of hotel life.

The summer was long, hot and busy. Towards September,
Jenny was looking forward to a little time to herself in her
comfortable little flat. She was quite stunned when a note arrived
from the management advising her that at the end of the season in
November her employment would be terminated. She had, of
course, been aware that the hotel closed for three months of the
year when she took on the post: in fact this had been part of the

attraction of the job – a three-month 'holiday'. But what Jenny had not read carefully enough was the small print at the bottom of her contract of employment, which stated, 'The management will be grateful if you would leave the flat in a clean and tidy condition when you vacate it on November 28th.'

Never, never take a job in middle age which has accommodation as part of the salary, without making *very* careful enquiries as to the tenure.

People on their own need to think even more carefully than do couples about a number of aspects of whether or not to move. A few examples of the points to consider before making final decisions about moving are:

1. Will you miss family and friends if you move? Maybe you will not miss the day-to-day contact, and will look forward to having visits from relatives and old friends? But remember that once the novelty of visiting you has worn off, these pleasant occasions may become fewer and fewer. It is surprising how lacking in interest erstwhile exciting events can become once there has been some time of absence. Also, both you and your friends will be getting older, and travel may become more difficult.

On the reverse side, you may be stimulated by the challenge of making new friends, and will gain much from new interests and faces. Only you can decide – but think carefully.

2. Is the new situation to which you are considering moving as convenient as the one you are proposing to leave? Will you miss the services of that helpful electrician down the road, who will mend broken appliances for you within 24 hours at minimum charge? And what about that young man who comes and helps with the garden? Doubtless there are equally helpful people in other parts of the country, but they have to be found. Are the local shops, library, church, dentist etc. as nearby as now? Maybe they are more so. But will this always remain the case?

• Muriel and Bob had moved from the suburbs of a large city into a small village five years before Bob's retirement was due. The village post office was the source of endless useful information and most of the everyday food requirements could be bought there. The church was just across the road and the hourly bus to the local town passed the door of the bungalow that epitomised all they had ever desired.

Bob took early retirement at 57, and settled down to replan the garden and join in village activities. But within three years, the village shop had closed, the church had only one service a month, and the bus service was reduced to one bus a day in each direction. The final decision to move back into the town came after a hard winter when the village was completely cut off for three days, the pipes froze and several slates were blown off the roof with disastrous consequences.

The moral is – do be careful that the status quo is likely to be maintained. (Check also that there are no plans afoot for a motorway to be built at the bottom of the garden.)

3. Remember that now you are retired – or approaching retirement – hobbies and entertainment will fill a larger part of your life. Check on the local facilities for your favourite pastime, and also on travel arrangements if they should be at a distance.

4. As mentioned earlier, moving expenses have a habit of mounting up in an alarming way. But once over this hurdle, do not forget to check on everyday housing expenses. For example, what are the rates on the new property that you are buying? Or is the rent likely to go up? What about ground rent, or service charges, if you are thinking of a retirement home?

5. What about your status if you move? Perhaps not something that you have much considered before? In your own home town you are known for the work you do and the leisure interests in which you join. But if you move away you will only be known as – perhaps yet another – couple/person approaching retirement. Maybe this will not worry you; in fact, maybe the challenge of making your mark will appeal to you. But think about it first.

6. Finally, what about health considerations? Should your

move take account of these? For example, is it advisable to move to a colder, damper part of the country if you are prone to rheumatism? Similarly, should your new home be in a hilly district if you have a heart or lung problem? If you do have any long-term health problems, check with your doctor about the advisability of your proposed move.

If you have been fortunate enough to own a holiday home in another part of the country, or maybe abroad, you will have to decide what to do with this property as you retire. There seem to be three options:

1. To keep the second home, and still visit it as hitherto as a place where you spend part of each year. Financial factors obviously have to be taken into consideration here. But if you can still afford to keep the property, remember that house prices will usually always rise, and so you will have an appreciating asset to sell at a later date if necessary.

Perhaps you could also make a little extra income by letting this property for certain times of the year when you do not wish to be there. Letting property to strangers for income can have its problems: non-payment of rent; being unable to repossess your own property if you need to do so; repair of damage done by tenants, to mention just a few. It is probably advisable, if you do own a holiday home, not to let on a commercial basis. Rather allow friends and members of the family to have the use of the property at a nominal fee just to cover electricity and other costs.

2. To move and live permanently in what was originally your holiday home. This will have to be considered as carefully as any other move. Are you sure that you will enjoy living there *all* the time? Fine for a much-needed break two or three times a year – but will you feel isolated and cut off in winter? The location of your second home will have a bearing on this facet, of course. Many places which on first sight would appear to be completely dead and devoid of activity and interest out of season, in reality come to life, in a different way, at these times. The local people organise

activities and outings and there is often much goodwill and friendship.

If you have been a constant, regular visitor, both in and out of season, you may well be warmly accepted into the community, and this option may be a very suitable one for you on retirement. The sale of your present house will bring in capital which can be invested either to buy extra income, or perhaps to alter your erstwhile holiday home to fit in with your permanent needs.

Again, think carefully before setting this option in motion – but for many people it can be ideal.

3. To sell the holiday home. Financial pressures may be such that this is necessary. Again, extra capital is made available by the sale – and maybe this was all part of your long-term retirement plans anyway.

A further possibility is to move locally – perhaps because the garden in your present home has become too much to cope with. But even a local move can have its possible problems, such as:

1. Will you mind seeing someone else in the house in which you have lived for many years? Changes will be made – you will probably be making changes to someone else's house – but do you want to be near enough to see them done?

2. Will you still be drawn to shop, or go to church, in the same way as you have done for many years when it is really so much more convenient to use the nearer, but not so familiar, shop around the corner from your new home? Perhaps not valid in your situation or for your personality, but nevertheless facets that need to be considered.

Taking a jump to the other extreme from moving locally, do your thoughts dwell on moving abroad, perhaps to a warmer climate? This is a possibility, especially for people who have children already resident in another country. Again, very careful thought must be given to this. A few questions to consider are:

1. Maybe there is a completely different lifestyle. Fine on holidays or short visits, but will you settle into the routine permanently? You will have to be a fairly adaptable, gregarious person to enjoy the challenge of permanent residence in another country.

2. Will there be a language barrier? If so, and you are unable to learn the language adequately or quickly enough, your social contacts may well be restricted to other expatriates. It also seems a little inconsiderate to settle in what is, after all, someone else's home land and make use of their better facilities (for example, a more congenial climate) and then not attempt to learn their language.

3. Pension arrangements will need to be looked into. The state retirement pension can be paid in any country of the world where you may choose to reside. Check carefully, however, that the country to which you are moving has reciprocal arrangements with Britain about the payment of any increases granted in retirement pension. If the country where you decide to move to does not have this reciprocal arrangement, you will not receive any of the increases that are bound to occur over the years. The DHSS Overseas Office in Newcastle has a list of countries which offer reciprocal arrangements, so check with them.

The tax position, on both pension and other income, has to be looked into. This can be a complicated procedure. Basically, you are still liable to pay income tax if you spend more than six months of the year in Britain, or more than an average of three months over four consecutive years. You are also liable if you still own a house/flat in Britain and use this – even for only one day. It is wise to get competent financial advice before moving abroad permanently.

4. Availability, and standard, of medical care. If you have private health insurance, this may not cover care abroad. Remember that few, if any, countries have a National Health Service comparable to that in Britain. Medical insurances with various companies and British provident associations provide health cover

abroad. Local insurance cover may also be available in the country to which you are going, but it is often expensive and less comprehensive than the insurance available in Britain.

5. Will you want to return to Britain when you reach your seventies? If so, remember that house prices will probably have risen out of all proportion by this time, and you may have difficulty in finding a suitable property. Living in a country with a cheaper standard of living can, for some people, be an encouragement to save money, but do not be misled into thinking that this will necessarily keep pace with inflation in the United Kingdom.

For some, and particularly well-travelled, people, this may be an ideal retirement pattern. But do give special thought to long-term aspects.

It is possible, of course, that this move – as you retire or approach retirement – will not necessarily be the last move you will make. Consider the possibility of two moves: one now for the active phase of your retirement (which could last for up to 15 to 20 years, a sizeable portion of your life, so it is important to get it right), then a further move into a different type of accommodation for your less active years. The needs of these two phases will probably be very different. Moving house can be upsetting, even traumatic, especially when you are older, but this drawback must be carefully weighed against the needs you have now and the needs you will have in 15 years or so.

Of recent years, more specific account has been taken of the need for retirement homes, tailor-made to the requirements of older people. Housing associations, formed with this idea in mind, are to be found in many parts of the country. Many such homes consist of one- or two-bedroom flats, and can be bought at a comparable price for a similar sized property in a similar area. Advantages are that they are built with possible health problems in mind – for example, single-level living, non-slip flooring, aids in the bathroom and so on. Obviously standards and facilities will vary between different associations and care must be taken when considering these. Frequently a site manager is available to give help if required.

Maintenance and care of surrounding lawns etc. are usually an integral part of the package. But check carefully both on the price you will be paying for these services and what exactly they will include.

'Mobile' or 'park' homes are also available in many parts of the country. Here, a number of prefabricated homes are built on special sites, each having a small plot of land, and sold at a competitive price. You can buy as large or as small a home as you require – mobile units can be fastened together to double the size. The price will depend much on the site: in general terms, homes on the South Coast are about three times as expensive as those in the north of England.

Check carefully on local facilities such as public transport, shops and other amenities. However pleasant and cosy your new home may be, it is less than perfect if the nearest shop is a mile away.

People who need rented accommodation have different problems. Houses and flats for private rental are difficult to find, and most are supplied at present by local councils.

Exchanges of council accommodation are theoretically possible. For example, you may be able to exchange your present accommodation – unsuitable for you because of its size – for a smaller flat or house. (This has an added bonus, of course, in that a family with several children will be able to move into a house that meets their needs.) This exchange can be arranged privately by advertising in one of the local papers. Some local councils will have information on possible exchanges locally, but this is by no means country-wide. It is obviously more difficult to arrange such exchanges if you are moving to a different part of the country, but there are a number of schemes which may be of help:

1. The National Mobility Scheme. This exists to help tenants move to a different region for special needs – for example, if you

have an elderly relative living in another part of the country and you wish to move nearer to be of help, this will be viewed sympathetically. Check with your local housing authority for details.

2. The Tenant's Exchange System is specifically designed to assist in exchanges between different parts of the country.
Both these schemes, of course, have to take into account the local housing lists – many of which stretch interminably into the future. But it is certainly worth making enquiries.

3. The Department of the Environment has a series of booklets on housing, available from the Citizens Advice Bureau or from your local council. One of the booklets is entitled 'Wanting to Move?' and includes information on accommodation both for rent and for sale.

Even with help, exchanges are difficult to arrange, but not impossible. It is certainly worth making enquiries.

So much for moving away from your present home. If you own your own home, what about staying where you are, and adapting your large house to your present needs? Maybe even using it as a source of added income if this is a particular problem?

1. Use the space available to maximum advantage. The rooms that used to be the children's need no longer be kept as bedrooms. Why not turn one of them into your own study/DIY/sewing room into which you can retire to 'do your own thing'. Within reason, it will not be necessary to clear up every time you have finished whatever you are doing – just shut the door on the carpentry/ sewing and no one will be the wiser. And how good it will be the next day to pick up the threads of the work exactly where you left off.

2. Other adaptations which will lead to your comfort will include a review of heating and insulation. Think about double glazing, loft and cavity insulation, if you have not already done so. You may be eligible for a grant to assist you financially on loft insulation: your local council will give you details – a leaflet

entitled 'Save Money on Loft Insulation' is available. Measures to lower your fuel bills will pay for themselves in the long run, and health benefits will be an added bonus – warmth is an important factor as we get older.

There are also other grants available from your local council, covering improvements that will bring your home up to a certain standard. For example, if you do not have an adequate indoor bathroom or toilet, or if you have a disability which prevents you from using an upstairs bathroom, you may well be eligible for a grant. Older houses – built before 1919 – can also qualify for a repair grant to bring them up to modern standards. These grants will not pay the whole cost, but will go some way towards helping with the expense.

While you are considering major adaptations to your home, think about other changes which will add to your comfort and ease of use – and which will also reduce your living costs.

Is your kitchen as well planned as it could be for ease of use? Do you have to walk from cupboard to hob to working surface and so on many times a day? With a little careful thought – and possibly a minimum of outlay – you could reduce this daily 'mileage'. Split-level ovens can be a boon to someone with a bad back – and automatic ovens really come into their own when you go out on a day's visit to relatives or a place of interest. There is nothing like having a meal cooked ready to serve to complete the day's enjoyment.

Combined fridge/freezers, too, are probably of more use during the retirement years than a separate fridge and chest freezer. Chest freezers are fine when they are needed to be filled with 'ready meals', pizzas, ice-cream etc. to feed a hungry family when they come in from work or school. But now a smaller cubic capacity is probably quite adequate for your retirement needs. As well as the convenience of searching for food in a smaller space, it is pointless spending money to freeze large quantities of air in a half-empty chest freezer.

Microwave ovens can also be a good investment if you find

yourself frequently needing to prepare a quick meal when you come in from an outing. They are not difficult to use once the basic principles have been mastered. Other pieces of kitchen equipment you will probably already possess. But an enjoyable hour spent in a store that specialises in the most up-to-date appliances may open new horizons to you.

The major improvement in the bathroom would be the installation of a shower. As you get older, taking a shower is often easier than struggling to get into – and out of – a bath if you suffer from even a minimal amount of arthritis. Financial savings can be made, too, as less water is needed to be heated for a shower than for a bath. Modern showers are very efficient, and water temperatures are easily adjusted.

An electrically heated towel rail is also a boon in the bathroom, providing a constant background heat, as well as keeping towels warm and dry. This form of heater can also be switched off for periods when you do not want heat in the bathroom – a distinct advantage over towel rails which are part and parcel of the general heating system.

Carpet, carpet tiles or cork tiles will also add to your comfort in the bathroom. Take advice on the type of carpet to use in a bathroom: unsuitable carpet can get unpleasantly damp and – in the long run – rotten.

While thinking about bathrooms and kitchens, remember the safety aspects of these two most dangerous rooms in the house – as well as other possible danger spots. (Remember that the majority of accidents occur in the home, and that older people and children are high risk groups.)

- A robust step-ladder – preferably with a platform – is essential as you get older. No longer is it possible to balance – if it ever was – on a stool put on top of a chair to reach those highest shelves. These steps will be found to be invaluable in all kinds of places around the house and garden.

- Avoid dark spots on landings and stairs by improving the

lighting in these places. Bifocal glasses may be a necessity as you get older, and these can be hazardous as you ascend or descend stairs. Do not increase the risk of a fall by poor lighting.

• Polished floors can look superb, but remember how easily you can slip on them – as well as, of course, the effort needed to keep them looking immaculate. Consider carpeting the whole of your house if at all possible.

• The bottoms of baths and showers can be slippery unless specially treated. If they are not treated, use a rubber bath mat to stand on. Dry skin needs bath oil, but the use of this can increase the possibility of slipping.

• Kitchen hazards are burns from cooking equipment and utensils, and cuts from sharp knives. Make sure your knives are kept safely, and always cut downwards on to a firm surface. Make sure that electrical equipment is safe – to avoid both electrocution and burns. (This applies to electrical equipment anywhere in the house. Check on the wiring of your house as well as leads on all electrical apparatus.)

• Still in the kitchen – is this where you keep any tablets you may have to take? Perhaps lined up on the window-sill? Fine as an *aide mémoire*, but not so good if you have small grandchildren visiting who are eager to explore and try anything within reach. All medicines should be kept out of sight in a cupboard – preferably locked – but certainly high enough to be out of reach of small exploring fingers. Check, too, that you have no out-of-date tablets around. These should be either returned to the pharmacist or flushed down the toilet.

3. If the financial cost of keeping up your home is a problem, but you feel disinclined to move, why not let out one or two of your spare rooms, on either a long-term or a short-term basis? Perhaps you have a mobile student population near you? Not all students are troublesome. A high proportion of youngsters are sensible, kindly folk who may be glad of a 'home from home' for a few

months, and there are mature students who would welcome the peace and quiet of an ordinary home. Check with your local college or university if this idea appeals to you.

Again, why not try setting aside a couple of rooms for bed and breakfast letting? – especially if you live in a popular part of the country. Many good friendships have been made, and cemented, by families coming back year after year.

A word of warning, however, if you are considering long-term letting of either a room or a flatlet into which you have made part of your house. It is far easier to let this accommodation than it is to get someone out who proved unsatisfactory for some reason. People who keep late hours, have noisy parties or entertain suspect friends in part of your house are definitely not what you were looking forward to in your retirement.

But perhaps as a long-term arrangement, consider turning part of your house, if it is too big for you now, into a self-contained flat. You may be able to get financial assistance with any necessary work from a Home Improvement Grant: check with your local council. You will be received with open arms if housing is in short supply in your area. Be sure, however, before you set out on this course of action, that you have a proper legal arrangement as regards what is expected of both parties to the agreement.

With all aspects of letting other people into your home, get adequate advice. The Citizens Advice Bureau can help, as can a solicitor. Chances are high, if you prepare carefully, that all will go smoothly to everyone's mutual advantage.

4. Home Income Schemes. Age matters here: you must have reached your 70th birthday before you can even consider this particular option of using your house to provide more income. There are, at present, two basic schemes available:

a) Mortgage Annuity Scheme. A mortage is arranged on your property and the money is used to buy an annuity for you. Income (taxable!) will be paid to you regularly for the rest of your life. The house will still be yours, so you will still be able to leave it to your children. They would have to sell the house to pay off the loan, but the remaining capital would be theirs. Consideration must be given to the type of agreement entered into, i.e. 'capital-protected' or a 'non-capital-protected' annuity. Be sure to get good advice before doing this. You cannot enter into this form of agreement until you are over 70, anyway. If your circumstances alter and you find that later on you have to live with relatives or be cared for in a residential home, the loan can be redeemed at any time.

b) Home Reversion Scheme. Here your house is sold. You retain the right to live there for the rest of your life together with either regular income payments or a lump sum. You will be expected to pay a nominal rent and will be responsible for the upkeep of the property. Certain insurance companies and building societies offer these options. Both schemes must be very carefully considered; they will certainly not be courses you need to consider as you are coming up to retirement age, or when you have just retired, rather something to be borne in mind if you are concerned, at times, about your long-term future.

One final word before leaving the housing scene – security, regrettably an increasingly necessary consideration today. Burglaries – often associated with violence – are frequently reported items in the news bulletins. So do be sure that you have done all that is possible to keep your house secure. A few points to look at will include:

● Doors. Are both front and back – and maybe also patio – doors capable of being securely locked? (And, most importantly, do you check that this is done every time you go out?)

Do you have a chain/spy hole on your front door, so that you can see who is there without the risk of an unwanted caller pushing in? A light over both back and front doors is an advantage so that you can see more readily who is there.

Patio doors in particular can be vulnerable. They are usually at the back of the house – out of sight of neighbourly eyes. They are also relatively easily forced unless you have taken the precaution to fit extra locking devices – or bolts to the older style french windows.

● Windows. Extra locks here are also a good investment. Venetian blinds can easily be moved aside by an intruder, but have the advantage of making a noise as they are moved, so if you are in the house you will be aware of the potential threat and can take action by dialling 999. Double glazing is also a good deterrent to the opportunist thief.

All these aids are, however, useless if you go out and leave a window open.

● Alarms of various types can be fitted. This is a specialist's job, and they are expensive. Advice on the most appropriate type can be obtained from the crime prevention officer at your local police station.

● Time switches to turn on lights at various times when you are away can be beneficial. These will not deter the determined thief, who perhaps has had your house under surveillance for a period of time, but the occasional, opportunist thief will pass your house by if a light comes on.

● A barking dog is also a great deterrent to opportunist thieves.

● High fences or prickly hedges are also helpful in making life difficult for the passing intruder.

● Neighbourhood Watch Schemes have recently increased in popularity on the crime prevention scene. These schemes are run in conjunction with the local police. Basically, one person in a road or a group of houses volunteers to act as co-ordinator. Each house in his 'patch' will be provided with a door-sticker stating that the house is part of the neighbourhood watch scheme. Also, each house is provided with an incident card. If at any time, anyone notices anything suspicious such as, for example, a strange car or van parked over a period of time nearby, a stranger knocking at the door, a stranger seen going to a neighbour's house when the watcher thinks, or knows, that they are away or out, or any other circumstances unusual to the neighbourhood, this card is completed and passed to the co-ordinator who in turn takes this to the local police station.

Of course, if anyone sees events which indicate that a crime is about to be committed, they must dial 999 immediately.

With the help of the information on the incident cards the police, in various parts of the country, have been able to build up a picture of suspicious events in a neighbourhood, and so have been able to prevent crime and also to apprehend criminals. It is stressed that at no time should any member of the public attempt to challenge a suspected criminal.

In some areas where the neighbourhood watch scheme is running successfully, the crime rate has dropped by as much as 16 per cent. If there is not a scheme in your district, contact your local police. They will be pleased to give you details.

Housing is an important part of the retirement process, and needs careful thought if you are to gain the best possible advantages from your retirement. Unsatisfactory housing can affect health and your outlook on life as well as your pocket. So think carefully, and get it right for this stage of your life. Times and situations inevitably alter, and further changes may be necessary later, but at this important time, good, suitable housing can give rise to long-term happiness and benefits.

3 · Finance

Money is an important factor throughout life, and certainly does not cease to be so as retirement looms. In fact it is probably one of the greatest worries felt at this time. Will our income be sufficient for our needs? Will we be able to maintain the same standard of living? Will we be able to afford holidays/the car/hobbies? These are some of the questions that flood in during those early-morning wakeful hours.

To be entirely subjective about this matter, it is surprising how frequently one hears recently retired people remark that their monetary situation has worked out far better than they ever dreamed. But a more objective look at money matters is necessary now that retirement is here, or nearly so. Plans, of course, cannot be as precise as they were in earlier life. No one knows how long he or she is going to live, and so plans must, to some degree, be flexible. It is a very useful exercise to jot down on paper your own estimated outgoings, and see how this balances against what your income will be once you are retired. As an initial fillip to your spirits, list the areas where you will find savings as compared to when you were at work. For example:

1. No further National Insurance contributions to be paid. These cease for men at 65 and women at 60 at present. (This applies, of course, only to women who pay the full National Insurance stamp.) If you have retired before the usual retirement age you may or may not have to continue paying contributions. Up to 1975 it was necessary to continue paying National Insurance contributions, or obtain credits for contributions by attending the employment exchange, in order to obtain a full pension at 60 or 65. But now, whether or not you need to continue paying National Insurance will depend on your contributions record throughout your working life. If this is good – contributions having

been paid for a long time with no breaks – there may be no further contributions to pay to receive a full pension. Leaflets NI15 and NI42 explain this, but to get information about your own specific status, contact your local Social Security office, giving your National Insurance number. They will be able to advise you.

2. Tax will be less. As well as there being less available money to tax, there are tax concessions to be had when retirement age is reached if your annual income is below a certain level. Advice on this, and other aspects of tax, can be obtained from a number of sources:

a) Your local tax office. (Even if the tax office which normally deals with your affairs is some distance away, the office nearest to you will be able to give advice on your specific tax queries if you give them full details and sufficient notice.)

b) The local Citizens Advice Bureau often has a specific money advisory service.

c) An accountant. Even if you have not used an accountant for your tax returns before, it can be a good idea to obtain the advice of one at this time – just as a 'one-off' exercise.

d) There are a number of Consumers Association publications (Which?) on tax and other related subjects. These are available from the Consumers Association, Castlemead, Gascoyne Way, Hertford SG14 1LH.

3. Prescriptions for medication will be free. When you get a prescription from your doctor, simply tick the appropriate box and fill in the details on the back of the form. You will then not be charged the usual fee.

4. Travel – by bus, rail and air – shows a marked reduction once you have reached retirement age.

a) bus companies, both private and those run by local authorities, usually have reduced fares, and some may even be free. There may be certain restrictions: for example, no concessionary rates at peak travel hours. (But who wants to get up to catch the 8 a.m. bus when you are retired, anyway?)

b) British Rail have a Rail Card, at present costing £12 for one year, that allows you to travel at half price on ordinary tickets. Again, there are restrictions on certain trains and at certain times. Leaflets are available at British Rail stations giving up-to-date information. Train travel in Europe also carries substantial reductions if you apply to British Rail for a Europe Senior Card, costing £5. Again, check with British Rail for full details.

c) British Airways give a 30 per cent discount on flights within the UK at mid-week, provided there is a minimum stay of six days. This applies to flights to Northern Ireland and the Channel Islands as well as to mainland journeys. Ask at your travel agent, or write direct to British Airways.

5. Many theatres, cinemas, swimming baths, art galleries, stately homes etc. offer reductions. Local arrangements on these concessions vary. There may be restrictions as to times when these benefits can be used. For example, cinemas often offer half-price seats for afternoon performances only, swimming baths have a reduced fee at off-peak times (much more pleasant anyway). Admission to stately homes, museums and certain sports events may also have a reduced entrance fee. Watch out also for reduced charges at hairdressers, dry-cleaners and other service industries.

6. Expenses which were incurred just because you were at work. For example:

a) Travel. Only a few lucky people were paid an allowance for travel to and from their place of work, or lived within walking distance. Now that you need travel only when you want, this expense need not be a routine part of your budget.

b) Clothes. Many forms of work demand certain types of clothing – be it white- or blue-collar work. Some jobs have clothing supplied, or an allowance given for this purpose, but most do not. (It is not suggested that you go around in your very oldest clothes all the time: but you will certainly find that clothes last, in a smart condition, far longer when you are retired.)

c) Food. People out at work all day often need to buy

convenience foods because of the time factor involved in preparation of meals. These tend to be more expensive, so costs may go down slightly on this front also. But remember that this may not always be so if you have been used to having a main meal in a subsidised canteen. Entertaining friends to a meal can be one of the pleasures of retirement. Although this can also lead to extra expense, that will be, to some extent, offset when you are invited to a return meal.

7. You will no longer be paying into any savings schemes for your retirement. The time has now come to enjoy the benefits of all those years of saving. Insurances paid over the years will be maturing, and your concern now will be how best to invest this money.

That is the good news. The reverse side of the coin must be looked at equally objectively. But do not forget that by a few alterations in lifestyle, or by investigation of hitherto unexplored possibilities, you may be able to save in many of these areas. On the debit side of your monetary list must come certain basic essentials:

1. Rates. This expense is one over which none of us has any immediate control – apart from moving to a cheaper area, of course. Rent will also come into this category if you are living in rented accommodation. If you are on a low income, however, you may be able to get help in these areas of expense through the Housing Benefit Scheme. Your local housing department will be able to advise you.

2. Heating. Remember to include all forms of fuel that you use, coal, oil, gas, electricity. Remember, too, that as you get older, the chances are that you will need to keep the house at a higher temperature than you did when you were younger and out for much of the day. But look out also for ways of reducing fuel costs. Good insulation is a priority, but do not forget to investigate other savings, such as cheaper rate electricity offered for certain periods of the 24 hours by electricity boards.

3. Food and other essential household goods, such as cleaning

materials. Your eating habits will probably not change as you retire (except perhaps the different timing of meals), but never consider cutting down on food bills to save money. Adjust your eating pattern if you wish, but never go hungry.

These three areas of expenditure are absolutely essential. There are only certain major ways in which you can reduce these bills. For example, moving to a smaller house will cut down on your rates and heating costs. But even this requires careful thought and research. That bungalow which appears so much smaller than your present house may well cost as much in rates. Checking, too, on insulation is a wise precaution when considering a new property. Without good insulation, you may be spending out as much on heating as you were for a larger but better insulated house.

Other expenses which must also be included in your budget if you are going to enjoy retirement at all are:

4. Running a car. Remember, it is not just petrol and oil: bills for road tax, MOT (if appropriate), servicing, parking fees (or fines) and any necessary repairs need to be considered. Having your own transport has many advantages, particularly if the area where you live is isolated or has poor public transport facilities. Remember, too, that as you get older you will feel less inclined to wait in maybe cold and draughty bus shelters or railway stations than when you were younger. Also, any necessary visits to doctor or hospital – which have to be considered – are so much easier if your own transport is available.

So, having made the decision to retain your car, what can you do to keep expenses to a minimum?

a) Consider changing your car for one which has a better fuel consumption.

b) Change to a lower insurance grouping if you previously owned a car that attracted a high insurance rating. These two acts will lead to positive savings. But also consider learning something about elementary car maintenance yourself, and so save on these bills. (Be sure, however, that you really know what you are doing –

it is never worth running the risk of an unroadworthy vehicle just to save a few pounds.) Basic car maintenance courses are available at most local adult education institutes.

Renting a car when necessary could be a further option open to you. But this can be inconvenient, particularly in not having a vehicle immediately available for emergencies. Also, a hired car will be unfamiliar to you, and remember that it is easy to get out of practice if you do not drive very frequently. Not that one ever forgets the skill completely, but reactions may be slower than previously for an initial hour or two.

If you have been a two-car family up to retirement, you could save a good deal of expense by giving up one car. (A useful sum of money for investment is also made available by this means.) But do think carefully before doing this. Is one of you going to be irritatingly restricted if your husband/wife will be using the car daily for part-time work or other pursuits? Discuss all aspects of this potential financial saving before making a final decision.

Driving licences last until the seventieth birthday. After this age your licence can be renewed for three years if you are medically fit, after 73 it must be renewed every year and must be supported by a doctor's certificate of fitness to drive. Your doctor is entitled to charge for this certificate – the recommended BMA fee at present is £20.

Transport can be an increasing problem as you get older – and also as public services deteriorate – so do think carefully before parting with your car. It will be very expensive to replace if you change your mind.

5. Leisure activities should also be included in your budget. Whatever interest you decide to spend more time on – or to start – it will cost you money to a greater or lesser extent. (See Chapter 7 for suggestions on new, or extension of old, hobbies.) Take gardening as an example. The actual land will be costing you nothing if it is part of the property that you own anyway. But consider the money you have spent over the years on plants, seeds, potting compost and so on, not to mention possible heating costs for the greenhouse or

the replacement of old and worn-out tools. Very few people these days cut their lawns with a hand-mower: the petrol or electricity involved in keeping a neat lawn also has to be considered.

Holidays should be included in your calculations. Even though to people who are still at work retirement seems like one long holiday, this is not, in practice, the case. Routine chores still need to be done, and many people find that they are working extremely hard after retirement. So holidays are just as important. In this field retirement can have positive bonuses. Now you can venture further, for longer. Holidays can be a positively enjoyable experience, rather than a time when energies need to be recouped. Time is also yours in which to plan in detail journeys to places you have always wanted to visit. Or perhaps you feel that now is the time to join in a specialist activity holiday – painting, archaeology, creative writing for example. (See Chapter 7 for further details.)

6. An 'emergency fund' should form part of your budget. No one can tell when the roof will leak, the washing machine blow up or the need for help in redecorating the house will arise. If these, and similar items, are neglected, or not replaced, the costs will increase as the years go on. Ideally, in your pre-retirement plans you will have considered renewing old, potentially worn out, pieces of household equipment. But no machine or structure lasts for ever without some degree of maintenance – and this, of course, has to be paid for.

7. If your company paid into a private medical scheme this will cease as soon as you retire. You will have to decide whether you want – or are able – to continue these payments. These schemes provide centres, in many large cities, where you can have a complete health check, costing at present around £150 for a two-hour session. This will be cheaper if you already subscribe to a private health scheme. Maybe you will wish to consider this option of checking on your health from time to time.

8. Any left-over mortgage payments will also have to be part of your calculations. Many mortgages are paid off by retirement, but with earlier enforced retirements occurring, this may not be so and

could be a factor you have to consider. You will have to decide whether or not it is wise to pay off the remaining sum owing with part of the money you receive from your occupational pension. Every individual case is different, and you should take advice on your own specific circumstances, but in broad terms, if you are a standard rate taxpayer, it would be in your best interests to pay off your mortgage. If you are in a higher tax bracket, you probably would be best advised to retain your mortgage, or at least some part of it.

This will cover most items of the average retirement budget. Each person and family will have different ideas on how best to apportion their available money. It is in the last five groups that you have room to manoeuvre.

YOUR PENSION

How your retirement income is made up will also obviously differ from person to person: there are probably no two pensioners who have their available money made up in exactly the same way. But there are broad categories from which money during the retirement years is derived:

1. State Retirement Pension. This is part of the reason why you have been paying National Insurance all those years. The retirement pension is not a charity handed out by a benevolent government: you have worked for it all your life and are entitled to every penny.

Your state pension is dependent on your having paid sufficient National Insurance contributions throughout your working life. You will have to have paid, or been credited with, contributions for around nine-tenths of your working life in order to get a full pension. The way in which these contributions have been paid will vary according to the circumstances of your working life. For many people this will mean a regular amount deducted every week, or month, from their pay, but the self-employed will have had to have paid at the relevant rate during the years that they were self-employed. If you have ever been registered as unemployed during your working life, credits will have been given which will contribute towards your pension.

If, for any reason, you have not been credited with sufficient contributions to receive a full pension, the amount you receive will be scaled down in proportion to what you have contributed. But you must have contributed for at least a quarter of your working life to receive a state pension at all. If you are in any doubt about the amount of your contributions, contact your Social Security office with all your available details. They will be able to tell you how much pension you are entitled to.

Married women, who may have had long periods of time when they did not pay any contributions at all, or only reduced ones, will usually be classed as dependants on their husband's contributions. So – even if you are older than your husband – you will have to wait until he is of pensionable age (65 at present) before you receive any state pension. Recently, due to changes made to bring Britain in line with Common Market rules, women can claim for dependent husbands under certain circumstances: well worth making enquiries if you think you fall into this category. Do not forget those few years that you were working before you were married, or before you had a family, when you paid full contributions: you may be entitled to a small pension in your own right even if your husband has not retired. Also worth remembering is any contribution you paid during the time of the graduated pension scheme, which was based on National Insurance contributions paid between 1961 and 1975. You may be entitled to a small pension based on this.

Finally, do remember that you actually have to *claim* your pension. It does not just arrive, by magic, on your 60th or 65th birthday. About four to six months before this date, the DHSS usually send a claim form: if you have not received this by the time your birthday is three months or so away, contact your local Social Security office. You will lose pension if you do not claim. Pensions cannot be backdated.

The method of payment is a matter of your choice. Your

pension can be paid straight into a bank or building society account, or you can choose to collect it weekly from your nearest post office. State pensions are paid on a week-in-advance basis. The actual amount you will receive will vary from time to time in accordance with government policy.

The earnings-related, or additional, pension scheme started in 1978 and will mean a small increase in the amount of pension you receive. Some companies 'contracted out' of the scheme, and agreed to increase their occupational pensions to the amount that would have been received from the state. Yearly increases on these amounts are at a slightly higher rate than the quoted flat rate.

Supplementary Benefit is available for those people who have only their state pension to live on and are finding it difficult to manage. About a quarter of retired people are entitled to this extra sum of money every week, but a great many – about 1,000,000 – do not claim. Many feel they are accepting 'charity' if they do so – but how wrong they are. They have paid into a pension scheme all their lives, and are entitled to receive the full amount of benefit laid down, if they need it.

To discover whether you are entitled to supplementary benefit, call at your local Social Security office to make enquiries about your specific circumstances. (If you have capital savings of over £3000 you will not be entitled to this extra pension, and you can earn only £4 per week without this affecting your supplementary benefit. This and other aspects can be clarified when your full details are discussed.) Other allowances – for example, heating, care of an elderly relative or special diets which can be expensive – may also apply to your situation.

Remember, however, that all pensions, including the State Retirement Pension, are taxable. All your sources of income will be added together and taxed at the standard rate after deduction of personal allowances. When you reach 65 (or 60), the 'personal allowance' deduction is replaced by a more substantial 'age allowance', so be sure that you are aware of this as you approach that age. A leaflet, 'Income Tax and Pensioners' (IR4), is available at your local tax office – worth asking for a copy to be sure that you are receiving all possible allowances.

2. Your occupational pension, or pension from your employer, will obviously vary from company to company, although all company pensions must be comparable to some degree. As you plan your retirement and attempt to balance your 'retirement books', it is as well to refresh your memory on just what you will be entitled to under your company pension scheme. When you joined the company – perhaps many years earlier – retirement pensions were probably one of the last things you were interested in. So check with your personnel department, if you are still at work. They will help to guide you through the sometimes complicated maze of pensions.

Most pension schemes are calculated in similar ways. The amount you will receive as pension will be based on your final year's pay (or sometimes on the best of the last three years' salary). Calculations are worked out as a fraction of this pay multiplied by the number of years you have worked for the company. (If you are not yet retired, consider paying 'additional voluntary contributions' – AVCs. Many occupational schemes allow you to 'top up' your pension by this means. As with the other contributions, AVCs are tax free, so you will be receiving some help from the tax man by doing this. Some schemes also allow you to buy 'added years' if you will not be entitled to the maximum amount at retirement: well worth making enquiries about if you are a few years off retirement.)

If you have changed jobs over the years, and your pension rights have not gone with you into the new company's pension fund, there may be some pension due to you from the earlier jobs. If you are not sure about any entitlement you may have, and if you have lost touch with the administration of your previous pension scheme, the DHSS Records Division at Special Section A, Newcastle on Tyne NE98 1YU may be able to help you to trace them.

In addition to the weekly/monthly pension, most company

schemes also give the option of a one-off tax-free lump sum payment. Public employers – such as the National Health Service – have this lump sum as an integral part of the pension package, but in other companies the choice is yours. You can accept a lump sum and a lower pension, or no lump sum and a higher pension. There are points to be considered on both these options, but remember that once you have had that holiday of a lifetime, your new car or your dream bungalow, by spending your lump sum, it is gone for good. Also, many pensions are 'index-linked', i.e. they increase with the cost of living. So, if you trade in part of your pension for a lump sum, you will lose this benefit on that amount of money.

But again, if you think you can afford to, why not start off your retirement years in an optimistic, happy frame of mind? – all part of the positive thinking process. Remember, too, that if you do not spend all of your lump sum, you must be sure to invest it wisely, so that it does not depreciate in value over the years due to inflation. (See later in this chapter for different forms of investment.)

Self-employed people will need to make their own arrangements for a pension scheme if they are to have any extra money coming in other than the State Retirement Pension. There are schemes run by insurance companies, which will vary in detail from scheme to scheme. But by retirement age it is to be hoped that you will fully understand all the implications of the scheme that you have been paying into for a number of years.

Advice on occupational pensions can be obtained from the Occupational Pensions Board, Lynwood Road, Thames Ditton, Surrey KT7 0DP or from Company Pensions Information Centre, 7 Old Park Lane, London W1Y 3LJ.

3. Further income for your retirement can come from your savings over the years if you have managed to put aside a little money regularly. Now is the time to review these savings, and perhaps reinvest them in something that will give you a regular income. However small this may be, it is surprising how every pound adds up when arriving regularly.

4. Paid work in retirement can also add to your income, but you must be careful that you do not lose some of your state pension rights. Your pension will not be affected if:

a) you only have an occasional job – for example, standing in for a friend or colleague for a week or so while they go on holiday;

b) your earnings are low;

c) the job you are doing is classed as part-time. This must be clearly defined in each case, but usually means working for less than 12 hours a week.

This 'earnings rule' applies to men between 65 and 70 and women between 60 and 65. So the amount you can earn before your pension is reduced is small. The reduction is gradual but will eventually be pound for pound. When you reach 70 if you are a man, or 65 if you are a woman, you can earn a higher amount without your pension being affected.

So do not dash into a three-day-a-week job once you have reached retirement age – after all, you deserve some rest and relaxation – without considering the financial implications. The situation will of course be different if you have retired early, as the state pension will not be involved, but your tax position must be thought about carefully – there is no benefit to you in working for the tax man. Rather you should consider taking up some form of voluntary employment which you will enjoy, and which will also be of much benefit to the community.

If you choose to carry on working full-time after retirement age, you can earn extra pension rights. If you work for an extra five years after the normal retirement age, the amount of pension you finally receive will have increased by almost one-third. No further National Insurance contributions will have to be paid in these circumstances: obtain a 'certificate of age exemption' from the DHSS. You can change your mind at any time about continuing work. So if after one year's work after the age of 60 or 65 you decide that you really have had enough, you can then claim your pension, having earned yourself a small increase in the meantime.

INVESTING YOUR MONEY

These then are the two sides of your financial accounting. With a little give and take here and there, most people manage to survive retirement in good financial shape. There is one aspect of the subject, however, that can cause problems – and perhaps many worrying hours as to whether you have pursued the best possible financial course. This is the problem of how to invest large sums of money. These could be from a lump sum payment or the maturation of an insurance policy, or maybe you think that you could invest your existing savings in a more lucrative way. Many options are open to you, and this aspect of finance can indeed be a difficult one to unravel. Talk to someone knowledgeable on financial matters, and with no axe to grind, about your own specific financial state if you can.

Everyone at retirement wants financial security. This security factor, linked to as high an income as possible, is the ideal situation at which to aim. Inflation is one of the difficulties here – how does one best guard against this fact of financial life? Perhaps the situation today is not quite as worrying as it was in the 1970s, when inflation rates were relatively high, but nevertheless inflation is a factor very much to be borne in mind as you plan your finances. Remember that even with a comparatively small 5 per cent inflation rate per year, the reduction in buying power in five years' time of a fixed income is 23 per cent, that is, £100 now will only be worth around £77 in five years' time, assuming inflation to remain constant. This also applies, of course, to your invested capital as well as to the interest gained on the sum. So it is important to look for some capital growth as well as a growing income from at least some of your investments. A good portfolio will contain some investments giving capital growth while others give a higher rate of income. Making risky investments in the hope of substantial gains should now be an activity of the past for the major part of your investment. But if you can afford a little money to invest in high-risk shares or unit trusts, for example, this can give many people an added interest and zest to life after retirement.

So, how should you plan your portfolio? The main structure is the same whatever size of lump sum you have to invest. Obviously, the larger the amount of money you have available the more you will be able to spread your investments and take calculated risks, but the principles are the same whatever sum you have to invest.

Basically, there are three main groups of investment that should make up your portfolio: variable interest investments, fixed interest investments and equity investments

Examples of variable interest investments are building societies, bank deposit accounts and National Savings. Capital sums here are secure, but take no account of inflation. Also, interest rates can vary so that your income – if you are relying on this interest – can drop overnight. This is a factor over which you have no control.

Ideally, some money should be in variable interest holdings – as security and to be readily accessible in emergencies. But do not have too much capital tied up here.

Examples of fixed interest investment are gilts, income bonds etc. Here you have the security of knowing exactly what your interest will be for a given term, but again these investments are subject to inflation – from both the interest and capital viewpoint. Also, if the money invested is needed in an emergency, you may lose capital on the sale of gilts before maturity because of market conditions and prevailing interest rates. (On the other hand, you could gain.) You would incur financial penalties by cashing insurance income bonds before the end of their fixed term. So again, some money invested here is sound policy, but remember the inflation risk and the possibility of being tied to a perhaps unrealistically low interest rate for a specific length of time.

Equity investments are shares quoted on the stock market, unit and investment trusts and so on. These investments offer the best chance of capital growth along with a rising income if the company invested in is doing well. But, of course, there is a much higher rate of risk in this form of investment, particularly in the capital part. This can be disadvantageous if you need to realise your capital in an emergency – the time when you need the money may not be the best time to sell. Unless the company – or the stock market – is overtaken by a disaster, your dividends (the interest earned on your capital) will remain constant.

So: the positive investor should be looking for a mix of investments in these three main groups. If the balance is right, you will secure high income together with an increase in your capital which in turn will further boost your income. A suggested good mix would be:

a) 25 per cent variable interest;
b) 30 per cent fixed interest;
c) 45 per cent equities.

You will need to sit down and work out how much money you will be needing from your investments to maintain the standard of living that you want. Most retired people will need the maximum amount of income from investments. It is tempting because of this to invest the majority of available money in variable interest investments, particularly building societies – perhaps because they are such a familiar way of keeping one's money? But experience has shown that, in the long term, this leads to a fall in available money mainly due to inflation and the variable interest rates. So do consider carefully the other forms of investment. It may be worrying initially to take the plunge into buying gilts, unit trusts or other forms of equities if you have never been used to putting your money anywhere other than in a building society or bank deposit account. Do it gradually, perhaps with the advice of a knowledgeable friend. Over the years you will appreciate the financial benefits and – who knows? – you may actually enjoy after a while this management of your financial affairs to the best advantage and become something of a financial wizard. The fortunes of your shares can be followed in the financial columns of your daily newspaper – and maybe you could one day make sufficient profit to pay for that exotic holiday you have always dreamed about.

Some further detailed notes on different investment possibilities may help you decide on your plan of action. But remember that a little good financial advice applied to your own specific set of circumstances is – quite literally – often worth its weight in gold.

VARIABLE INTEREST INVESTMENTS

1. Building Societies. There are many and bewildering choices offered by the increasing number of High Street building societies. Recently, owing to intense competition from other available investment options (and other building societies), they are offering a high rate of interest on some accounts. Guaranteed higher rates are offered over the ordinary share rate for definite periods. The only disadvantage is that penalties can be incurred if you wish to withdraw capital without giving the required period of notice. (The amount of notice to be given varies, but 30 or 90 days are examples.) So – emergencies excepted – this can be beneficial if you plan well ahead for any capital you may need. 'Term shares' *cannot* be withdrawn before the agreed time has elapsed, so this type of building society investment must be thought of as a long-term one.

Tax on building society accounts is deducted at base rate before you receive your interest. This deducted tax cannot be reclaimed, so if your income is such that you do not pay tax, building societies are not a good investment.

Advantages:

Money is readily accessible, the only disadvantage being the penalties incurred by early withdrawl on some accounts.

High rate of interest available.

Regular income payments can be made – or, alternatively, you can arrange to withdraw interest at six-monthly or yearly intervals.

Disadvantages:

No protection against inflation.

Deducted tax can be disadvantageous in some circumstances.

2. Bank Deposit Account. Interest rates here are not as good as those given by building societies and and are linked to the bank

rate, so they will, of course, vary with this. Higher interest rate deposit accounts are available, but these require a certain minimum investment – usually £1000. As with building societies, your money is readily available and interest can be transferred to your current account as you wish. Tax is deducted at source at base rate.

Advantages:

Your money is safe.

Your money is readily available.

Disadvantages:

Interest rate comparatively low and can vary.

No protection against inflation.

Recently a 'high interest cheque account' has been floated by many of the main banks. Here higher interest rates are offered (in line with those offered by the building societies), together with the advantages of a cheque book and, in many cases, credit card facilities also.

3. National Savings. National Savings Income Bonds offer a competitive rate of interest, and can be used to pay a monthly income. Interest is paid without deduction of tax, so this form of investment is useful for the non-taxpayer. Capital growth is not possible with this form of investment. The bonds cost £1000 each and the minimum investment is £2000. To recoup your investment you have to sell a complete bond or multiple of bonds. Application forms can be obtained from your local post office, or by writing to NSIB, Bond and Stock Office, Blackpool FY3 9YP.

Advantages:

Your investment is safe.

On some types (index-linked National Savings), inflation is counteracted.

Return is tax-free after agreed term has been fulfilled.

Disadvantages:

Money is not readily available without incurring penalties.

No capital growth.

FIXED INTEREST INVESTMENTS

1. National Savings Certificates. These offer a fixed interest rate over a four- or five-year period. For example, the 29th issue – Autumn 1984 – has an agreed rate of interest of 8 per cent. This is only applicable if the certificates are held for the full five years. (You can, of course, cash your certificates earlier in the case of an emergency, but interest is lost.) The return is tax free after the agreed term has expired.

Index-linked National Savings Certificates are also available. Interest is not paid, but their value is guaranteed by the government to keep pace with inflation. After five years there is also a 4 per cent bonus. Worth considering if you have a sum of money you will not be needing for five years.

2. Gilt-edged Securities. These are fixed-interest stock issued by the government for an agreed term. Local Authority Stock works in a similar way. By holding your chosen stocks until they mature you have a positive income guaranteed as well as a known capital value on redemption. The income is usually a little lower than that offered by building societies, but is fixed, so if any disaster befell building societies whereby interest rates plummeted, gilts would be the better investment.

The time in which the stocks mature varies – anything from one to thirty years. Obviously you will need to take into account all your other investments to decide which stock is best for you.

You can buy these stocks through a stockbroker, through your bank or by obtaining a form from the Post Office (the National Savings Stock Register). This latter register is comparatively limited, but it can accommodate most requirements, as it has around fifty stocks available. The advantage of dealing on the National Stock Register is that costs are lower. Both banks and stockbrokers charge a fee for the transactions. Also, if stocks are bought through a bank or a stockbroker, tax is deducted at source; with a Stock Register transaction interest is paid gross, which for people on a lower income means that they do not have to reclaim the tax.

Any capital gain made on the sale of gilts is free from capital gains tax.

Some unit trusts specialise in gilts, but, of course, these are subject to management charges on the fund. Investing in gilts by this method removes the burden of decision from you, and if the management is competent you should more than cover this cost by their insulating you from the effects of interest rate swings on your capital.

Advantages:

Known fixed income for a given period.

Gains can be made, by both capital increase (free of capital gains tax) and high income.

Disadvantages:

Money tied up for a definite period.

Inflation can reduce value of capital and income. (Index-linked gilts are also available, but interest rates are low.)

3. Annuities. These are a form of fixed-interest investment in which a once-for-all payment is made – which is non-returnable – in exchange for a fixed income for life. No tax is payable, as the income is deemed merely a repayment of capital. Inflation can seriously erode this fixed income, and this form of investment is not a good idea if the chances are high that you will be needing this income for another twenty years or so. For people over 75 this option may be more suitable.

Advantages:

No tax payable on income.

Worry-free investment for the over 75s.

Disadvantages:

Inflation erodes value.

Loss of control of capital.

Other forms of temporary annuities run for a fixed period of time. This can be useful to bridge a gap when you know your income is going to be low – for example, if you retire early and have a few years to wait before receiving any form of pension.

EQUITY INVESTMENTS

1. Unit Trusts. Basically, these trusts manage a portfolio of shares: instead of yourself dealing in shares in various companies via the Stock Exchange, the unit trust will do this for you. Investment will be made in a wide range of shares so as to reduce risk.

Income unit trusts are a good choice. There are two types of these trusts. One gives a higher starting income by investing in preference shares, convertibles and other fixed interest investments as well as pure equities, but the scope for future growth of capital and income is limited. The other type of income trust invests solely in good quality equities. These give a lower initial income, but the scope for growth of capital and income is much greater. Compared with building societies, unit trusts are superior, both as regards capital and income appreciation as long as you can afford to be patient, accepting a lower initial interest rate. Obviously, the longer you leave your money in a unit trust the greater will be the gain.

Dividends (or interest) are usually paid twice a year. If you need a regular monthly income, you could purchase a number of different trusts which pay dividends at different times of the year. The progress of your unit trust can be followed in the financial columns of your daily newspaper.

Advantages:

Good income and capital growth over the long-term.

Risks limited by a good spread of shares.

Inflation less of a problem due to both capital and income growth.

Disadvantages:

Interest will initially be lower.

Capital value may fall at times, so if you need to sell at these times, a loss could be incurred.

More information on unit trusts can be obtained from the Unit Trust Association, Park House, 16 Finsbury Circus, London EC2M 7JP.

2. Shares. These are investments bought in individual companies, and can be risky for the non-professional investor. To reduce the risk, a wide spread of shares should be bought, and it is necessary to have a fair amount of capital available to do this. You will need good advice before venturing into this form of investment.

Advantages:

Gains can be made if shares are bought and sold at the right time.

Can be of great interest if you have that sort of mind – and a little knowledge.

Disadvantages:

Risks are high if investments are unwise.

You will need at least £10,000 to invest. Amounts less than this are too risky if this is your sole form of investment.

There are other specialised forms of investment in which you can put your money, such as unit-linked insurances and specialised deposit accounts, and income can be raised from the equity of your home (see Chapter 2 for further details). But for all these investments you would be well advised to consult your accountant or a stockbroker.

Investment of a capital sum of money in the best possible way can be fraught with difficulties, and, as mentioned before, a knowledgeable, uncommitted friend to give advice can do much to help with your decisions. Whatever you do, remember that your investments should never cause you to lose any sleep. If they do, move your money somewhere else – it is at too much risk where it is.

MORTGAGES

Ideally, everyone's mortgage will be paid off fully by the time they retire, but with today's – possibly enforced – early retirement, this may not always be the case. The question then arises whether to pay this sum off altogether or to retain it until the due time. Each individual case will vary, of course, and it is wise to take professional advice on the advisability of what to do in your specific situation.

Basically, if you are a standard rate taxpayer, it is probably in your best interest to pay off the remaining sum owed with part of the lump sum you have received from your pension, but if you pay a higher rate of tax, the tax relief gained on continuing mortgage payments will be advantageous. The amount of income you need from investments also comes into the calculations here. Perhaps paying off part of your mortgage will be the best compromise in your particular situation.

INSURANCE

What about your insurances? Not the kind which are now providing you with your pension, but insurances on your property, its contents and any valuables that you may have. It is most important that your goods are fully insured: it would be even more difficult to replace them now that you are on a fixed income than it was when you were working.

First of all, check on the house insurance – for the actual building. Probably this was automatically done by the mortgage company when you still had a mortgage, and renewal notices arrived regularly to remind you: now it is up to you. Index-linked policies are the safest, but it is still important to check at intervals that the sum insured really would bear the total cost of rebuilding if there were to be a catastrophic fire and your whole property were burnt down.

Then contents. Have you recently added up the replacement value of all your household belongings? If not, do so, and it will surprise you just how much it would cost to replace many of the items. Not that the sentimental value can ever be replaced, of course, but at least it is good to know that you would be able to replace the household necessities if they were stolen or destroyed. Make sure, too, that you have a clause 'new for old' in the insurance policy on your goods. The premium will be slightly higher, but is well worth the extra cost. It is also worth comparing the deals offered by various insurance companies: premiums can vary as much as 50 per cent in some cases, for the same type of cover.

Life insurance will not have the same importance now that your children are no longer dependent on you, but many people still wish to have some form of life insurance cover to ensure that their spouse is well provided for when they die.

Whole life policies pay the amount agreed on death to the named beneficiaries. Premiums are paid in the usual way, on either a monthly or a yearly basis. These are not particularly good value, and most folk needing this type of insurance decide on whole life policies with profits, where the beneficiaries get the sum assured plus added bonuses together with a terminal bonus. This form of policy is definitely the better option if premiums have been paid for ten years or so.

Premiums will be dependent on a medical examination – paid for by the insurance company with the doctor of their choice. If you are reasonably fit and well this should not prove to be a problem, but if you have some medical condition there may be added premiums to be paid.

Life insurance can be bought through a broker, through your bank or direct from an insurance company. Again, as with all financial matters, it is worth shopping around and getting the best deal you can for your own particular circumstances.

YOUR WILL

Making a will should not be a depressing thought – after all, it will not make one jot of difference to the date of your death. But leaving an up-to-date will can make all the difference to your relatives when this does occur. It is so much easier to sort out the financial affairs of someone who has taken the trouble to state exactly to whom, and when, they wish their money and goods to be left.

Retirement is a good time to settle down and evaluate just what you have to leave by way of money and goods.

Wills can be made yourself on a will-form purchased from a stationer's. But it is far safer, and more satisfactory, to ask a solicitor to draw up a will for you. The charge is small and, as well as benefiting from his advice, you will be absolutely sure that the legal position is clear. Make sure that your partner, your children or a trusted friend knows where your will is kept. A will can be lodged with a solicitor, at a bank or in your own home. It is advisable to use one of the first two options for reasons of safety – you can always keep a copy at home to refresh your memory of the contents should this be necessary.

It is usual to name executors to a will. They can be relatives, friends or an institution such as a bank. It is a good idea to appoint as an executor one of the beneficiaries, who will have good reason to make sure that all runs quickly and smoothly.

Leaving money and goods will, of course, be dependent on how much you have to leave and who you have to leave it to. One or two points should be noted concerning the bequest of money.

1. Inheritance tax is payable on most bequests and gifts. So the value of what you are leaving may be less than you think.

2. Certain exemptions from inheritance tax are worth remembering:

    a) Leaving your estate – money, goods, property etc. – to your husband or wife is exempt from tax. (But tax will have to be paid when the surviving partner dies.)

    b) Capital transfer tax is not payable on the first £90,000 (at present) of the assets you leave. But do remember that if you own the house in which you live, it is worth a sizeable sum of money.

    c) You can give away £3000 every year without paying tax. So it is worth considering, for example, giving your children a gift now and again if you can afford it.

3. Even if you think you have very little to leave, it is worth jotting down just what are your assets – house, furniture, car, life insurance policies, to mention just a few.

If you die intestate, there are definite rules about to whom your estate passes. For example, if you are married with children, a first set amount (this varies from time to time) and your personal effects go to your spouse and the remainder is divided, half going to your children and the remaining half being invested to provide interest for your spouse for life, the capital reverting to your children on her/his death. If you have no children, the first proportion (again variable from time to time) and half the remainder, together with your personal effects, goes to your spouse. The rest will go first to your parents, then to your brothers or sisters. Maybe this is what you would have wanted anyway, but then again it may not be. So do make your will soon if you have not already done so. It can always be altered at a later date if you wish.

Finance is a continuing problem throughout life, and it can become a burden during retirement. But with forethought and planning, this load can be eased so that you can look forward to making your retirement the best time of your life.

4 · Fitness

Before looking at how your health shapes up to the retirement years, what about your fitness? Yes! – fitness: by no means the same thing as health. Reasonable health is, of course, a prerequisite of fitness, but do remember that you can be perfectly healthy, but definitely unfit. (This applies throughout life – to teenagers as well as to those approaching retirement.) 'Health' means an absence of disease; 'fitness' means that all parts of your body are working at maximum efficiency.

It is only when your body is put to the test that you can definitely tell how fit you are. A fit and an unfit person sitting side by side are indistinguishable, but when they have to meet some physical challenge, such as running for a bus, the difference becomes apparent. If you are fit, your body will respond to the physical challenge of the extra exertion in several ways:

1. Your pulse and breathing rate will only be slightly raised.

2. You will not feel unduly tired or distressed by the extra exercise.

3. You will have no stiff joints or muscles the following day.

Put another way, remember the three S's of the fit person: STAMINA – STRENGTH – SUPPLENESS.

STAMINA

Stamina is the 'power of endurance'. In the context of fitness, this means how long you can continue a specific task or form of exercise without becoming too distressed by breathlessness and/or an unpleasantly rapid heartbeat. To increase your stamina you must train your heart and lungs into maximum (for you) working trim.

A note of caution must be sounded here for those people who suffer from heart disease, high blood-pressure or any long-term lung condition such as emphysema or chronic bronchitis. Before taking up any form of exercise you should check with your doctor, who will be able to advise you as to what type of exercise is best suited to your needs. But do remember that many chronic conditions can be improved by regular *suitable* exercise. These provisos will also apply to any exercise undertaken to improve your strength and suppleness.

But assuming you are fortunate enough to have a healthy heart and lungs, what should you do specifically to increase your stamina?

1. Check your level of fitness with regard to your heart and lungs first of all. Do this by:

running on the spot for 30 seconds,

then check your pulse rate. Do this by feeling the pulse in your wrist and count the beats for a quarter of a minute – 15 seconds – multiply this by four to calculate the beats per minute.

This should be between 100 and 120 in a reasonably fit person. (Athletes have a – sometimes incredibly – slow heart-beat. This shows that each beat of the heart is pushing out the maximum amount of blood necessary to oxygenate the tissues, so work is being done at maximum efficiency. It is doubtful that you, nearing retirement, will ever reach this peak of efficiency, but that is no reason for not trying.)

The figure you come up with is *your* personal exercise heart-rate.

2. You should now aim to be able to exercise (in the manner of your choice) for 10 to 15 minutes without your heart-rate exceeding this figure. If it does become higher after a few minutes of exercise, stop for a rest period. This must be for as long as it takes for your heart-rate to return to normal (76 beats per minute is the average normal resting pulse-rate in a healthy adult. Variation of 10 beats either way is within normal limits.) It is important that you

never exercise beyond your capabilities at any one time. This will not only overstrain heart and lungs (and probably also muscles and ligaments), but will do you absolutely no good at all. It doesn't have to hurt to be doing you good!

3. As your stamina improves you will be able to continue with your chosen form of exercise for as long as you wish without feeling distressed by either a rapid heart-beat or breathlessness. But do not expect this to happen all at once, particularly if you have allowed yourself to become unfit. Remember, too, that getting yourself fit should be an enjoyable process. You are not aiming to take on the world's athletes. The only prize at the end of the day is your own improved fitness. So be gentle with yourself, and build up your stamina in easy – but regular – stages.

STRENGTH

Strength is the power of your muscles. Under-used muscles will still fulfil the function of maintaining an upright posture and of movement, but without regular exercise these functions will be carried out less efficiently and certainly with a good deal of effort and discomfort. One has only to look at a gang of walkers after a five-mile ramble to pick out those whose muscles are working at less than 100 per cent efficiency. And it is not only the larger muscles of the body that are involved. Any pianist will tell you how stiff and uncomfortable their hands become if their practice has lapsed for a few days.

There are very many ways of improving the strength of your muscles – cycling, swimming, dancing, to mention just a few. But if your muscles are in poor trim, why not start off improving the situation by a regular walk *every* day? And this means a walk, not a stroll! Perhaps you have a favourite walk? – around the block? – across the nearest field? – or, if you are lucky enough to live by the sea, along the beach or cliff-top? Now that you are walking in an endeavour to strengthen your muscles, stride out – get your pulse-rate up – and do not slow down when your leg muscles begin to ache. Keep going for those few minutes longer. Get into a rhythm of walking fast, with long strides for a few yards – the distance between two trees or lamp-posts, for example. Then drop back to your basic slower pace for a few yards, and repeat the process again throughout your walk. As you increase pace, try also to expand your lungs to their fullest extent. This will also improve stamina. You will find that over the days and weeks, if you keep up this exercise regularly, you will be able to walk further and further without discomfort.

SUPPLENESS

Suppleness is the ability to move all your joints through their full range without pain, and without being crippled by stiffness the next day. (People with arthritis will obviously have difficulty in keeping their suppleness. But many arthritic conditions can be improved by appropriate gentle exercises – this is, after all, the basis of physiotherapy. If this applies to you, ask your physiotherapist to show you exercises that you can do yourself to help improve your suppleness.)

Check on your degree of suppleness in each of your major joints in turn. If you find any excessive stiffness in any particular joint, endeavour to improve this by putting the particular joint through its full range of movements each day.

1. *Ankles and feet.* Circle your ankles, both clockwise and anticlockwise. Stretch your feet to all parts of the compass. Do they creak and groan? Then practise this regularly for a few days during your 'sitting down' moments, and see the improvement in a couple of weeks in the range and suppleness of movement. Do not be surprised, however, if the creaks in these joints persist. Many healthy joints do this throughout life.

Straighten all your toes fully, and then bend them to their fullest extent. Impossible? Then gradually increase this range of movement day by day.

Try walking around the house on tiptoe. Not only will this

improve the arch of your foot, but it will loosen up the joints of your toes as well.

2. *Knees and hips.* Check for suppleness by marching on the spot, with knees well up at each step.

Lying on your back, and 'cycling' in the air with your legs will also tell you how supple are these particular joints.

Both of these exercises are helpful, if done regularly, in increasing the suppleness of knees and hips.

3. *Wrists, shoulders and neck.* Circle your wrists.

Stretch and bend your fingers as you did your toes. Unless you suffer from arthritis, these parts of your body will probably be in better trim than your larger joints. Most people use their hands fully, in many different ways, throughout their working lives.

But can you say the same for your shoulder joints? Can you reach up and clap your hands together over the top of your head – not six inches in front of your head, but right over the top? And what about arm circling? Is it really a good, wide swing, fully moving your arm through a wide circle? Shoulder joints are probably one of our most under-used joints – few of us need to reach fully upwards regularly.

Closely connected to shoulder joint movements are neck movements. A vast number of people have, to a greater or lesser degree, pain and stiffness in their necks. This is frequently due to changes – injury or ageing – in the bones and ligaments of the neck. Tension is then put on the muscles. A stiff, painful neck is the result, with often an associated throbbing 'tension' headache. Regular, gentle exercise of the neck can do much to reduce these painful symptoms as well as improving the general suppleness of the neck.

LONG-TERM BENEFITS OF FITNESS

1. However unlikely it may seem as you begin the long climb up to fitness – if you have become unfit over the years – you really will notice an overall improvement in your general feelings of wellbeing.

2. You will sleep better. There is nothing like regular exercise to improve sleep. As we get older our sleep pattern alters (see later in this chapter) and all too frequently this means, for many people, long, wakeful hours in the middle of the night.

• Marie and Jim were a couple in their early sixties who found this particular aspect of ageing a problem. If one partner was wakeful, it meant that the other was woken up – and that meant that they were both tired the next day. So they indulged in a nap in the afternoon, but soon found that was counterproductive, as they woke even more frequently in the night. The answer to the problem was found when a friend introduced them to ballroom dancing. They became so keen that they entered competitions and were dancing three or four nights every week. As well as adding interest to their lives by finding an activity they could enjoy together, Jim and Marie now have absolutely no problem at all with sleeping at night. As Jim put it, 'We both go out like a light for a good seven hours!'

3. Any tendency to overweight will be helped by the activities you undertake to improve your stamina, strength and suppleness.

4. You will develop a healthy appetite following your exercise. Not for you the frequent nibbling at – possibly unsuitable – food to pass the time. You will feel ready for meals, and, if they are properly planned, you will both enjoy and benefit from your food intake.

5. One of the more worrying aspects of getting older is lack of stability on your feet. Fractures of limbs – a common cause of hospital admission in older people – highlights this problem. Obviously visual and auditory problems have a bearing on this fact of life, but if your muscles and joints are in good working order you will be more able to avoid these kinds of problems.

6. Finally, by keeping your body fit you will keep yourself more mentally alert as well.

WAYS OF INCREASING FITNESS

Everyone can improve their fitness. But how, in detail, does one set about this? Remember that it is not just exercise to improve stamina, strength and suppleness that is necessary, but also a healthy diet, a good sleeping pattern and a regular check-through on your 'body maintenance' (see Chapter 5).

This may seem a formidable list at first sight, but to a large extent it is only what you have been doing – or *should* have been doing – for your body throughout life. You certainly checked on all these aspects of your children's health when they were little. Now the time has come to give a little thought to yourself.

Remember that health care must be pursued on a regular basis. It is no use checking on all aspects of your health and fitness, and then relapsing, with a sigh of relief, into those old habits of letting your body 'get on with it'. Keeping fit is hard work, but the benefits to be gained are immeasurable. After all, it is the *quality* of life that is of prime importance as retirement looms on the horizon.

A word here about disabled people – whether by arthritis, chronic heart or lung conditions or one of the other long-term illnesses that can afflict any of us. You too can improve your fitness. Remember that almost any long-term disability will usually lead to relative immobility and immobility is one of the worst enemies of fitness. Obviously, your exercise and diet patterns will need to be geared to your specific requirements, and specialised help and advice will often be necessary. But do not think that just because you have a long-term disability you are exempt from trying to improve your fitness. The benefits you could gain can be infinitely rewarding. But before starting on any course of action, check with your doctor as to the suitability of what you are proposing to do.

EXERCISE

A good deal has been written and spoken over the years about regular, suitable exercise. Magazine articles, books, television and radio programmes all applaud the benefits of exercise of various kinds. And it is true that regular, suitable exercise does benefit our bodies – and minds – in a variety of ways:

Levels of bodily fitness by way of stamina, strength and suppleness are only obtainable by regular exercise of one kind or another. Most younger people instinctively use their bodies to maximum effect – it is all part of their natural *joie de vivre*. But as we age, the desire to move our bodies vigorously declines. Pressure of time, commitments to family and career are all factors in this decrease in physical activity. And the less activity that is undertaken, the less is the desire to exercise the body. Joints become stiff, muscles protest at even minimal exercise, and heart and lungs become out of trim. So, for relaxation, we collapse into the nearest chair. Then anxiety about our unfit state can intervene, and an anxiety/inactivity cycle can too readily become the pattern.

It is only by making a determined effort to organise a regular routine of exercise that you can break this cycle. It will be hard at first, but the long-term effects will be well worth your trouble.

Go to a keep-fit class for the first time, or start off on a gentle planned exercise course, and you will be surprised by how good you feel afterwards. Almost as good as the feelings of physical wellbeing you used to feel after a good work-out in the gym when you were at school. (Even if you absolutely hated this particular part of the curriculum, you must admit to positive feelings of wellbeing afterwards? – and not entirely due to feelings of relief that the whole horrible procedure was over!) This is not just in the mind. Physical exercise releases certain hormones into the bloodstream that affect your state of mind. Feelings of tension and stress are released, and life is viewed in an altogether different light.

Exercise not only 'makes your heart grow stronger', as the health education leaflet tells us, it is one of the ways in which you can help yourself reduce the risks of a heart attack. During exercise the body's metabolism (the ways in which our food materials are handled) is improved. Cholesterol levels are reduced during exercise, and excess carbohydrates are burned up. High levels of certain fats and sugars are thought to have a bearing on the incidence of heart disease. Inactive bodies do not burn up the excess amounts of these substances that we are all inclined to eat.

Posture has a large effect on back pain. Regular exercise will improve the strength of muscles which fulfil the vital role of holding your back in a good position. Take a look at yourself in the mirror, sideways:

Are your shoulders rounded?

Does your stomach stick out?

Does your chin jut forward?

If so, try straightening up and see the difference. Maybe your muscles will be crying out in protest after a few minutes of holding this posture? If so, a few back exercises – gently at first, but certainly on a regular basis – should be your plan.

Brain activity, by way of loss of memory and slowness of response, is always thought to be associated with the ageing process. But this is not inevitable. Remember Winston Churchill (whose finest work was done close to the usual retirement age), and a host of other people whose minds are as keen as those of many younger men and women. Keeping your mind active is of prime importance in this context, but exercise, too, has benefits on mental activity. The blood supply to the brain – carrying vital oxygen – is increased during exercise, so brain function will benefit. Also, while you are concentrating on your chosen form of exercise, you cannot be feeling anxious, panicky or depressed. Interaction with other people pursuing the same form of exercise will also be of enormous importance in keeping your mind on top form, as well as combating loneliness.

TYPES OF EXERCISE

The list of possible ways of taking – and enjoying – your daily exercise is long and varied. It ranges from the energetic sports such as tennis and squash, through ballroom dancing and cycling to less strenuous pursuits such as rambling, archery and bowls. You will, of course, be restricted in your choice by what is available locally, but if some particular sport (or indeed other interest) is not represented in your area, why not make enquiries about starting a group? It is amazing how many like-minded people you may find. Your local library, education centre or Citizens Advice Bureau are all good starting points. Writing to the national headquarters of the particular activity will also produce useful advice.

Before deciding what particular kind of exercise would interest you, check on the advantages to fitness of each specific activity. (Obviously, if you have been a keen rambler all your life, you will be searching out new areas to explore. Who knows, you may become a second John Hillaby, and commit your thoughts and adventures to paper.) Only a few of the possibilities are mentioned here, but perhaps you could make a similar check-list of bonus points for the sport or exercise in which you are interested.

Give 'bonus' points for:

any exercise which increases strength;

any exercise which increases stamina;

any exercise which increases suppleness;

any exercise which demands you use your brain.

For example (see table on p. 80 for scoring):

Rambling. The strength of your leg and back muscles will certainly be increased by this activity, but arms and shoulders will not benefit much. Stamina will be increased as you extend your range, especially if you keep up a fair pace for much of the way. Again, any increase in suppleness will be largely confined to the lower limbs. Mental agility will depend very much on what interest is taken along the way, and what companions join you on your rambles.

Squash/tennis. Strength and stamina score well on these two sports. Suppleness increase is limited to a specific range of joints. Mental agility is rated high as strategy is worked out. But remember that these two sporting activities, particularly squash, make great *sudden* demands on many parts of the body. For this reason it is as well to be careful at what level you play these competitive sports as you gain in maturity.

Cycling. As with rambling, strength is increased only in the leg muscles by cycling. Similarly, stamina will be increased in proportion to the vigour with which you cycle. You will notice, if you persist with this form of exercise, the greater ease with which you will cycle up that erstwhile seemingly unsurmountable hill. Again, suppleness is restricted to only those joints which move in cycling – knees, hips and ankles. One extra bonus of cycling is that the weight-bearing joints – hips in particular – are relatively cushioned from strain by the very nature of the sitting posture. This can be of benefit to those folks with minimal osteoarthritis (a condition due to 'wear and tear' on the weight-bearing joints). The joints are maintaining their suppleness without overloading their weight-bearing function.

Mental agility is a necessity in dealing with traffic problems these days. The risk of accidents is the major disadvantage of cycling. But if you are fortunate enough to live where you can easily get away from crowded roads, cycling could be for you. The territory covered in a day can be so much more than you are able to cover on foot.

Swimming gains good bonus points in all aspects of fitness, with the exception of the mental demands made. It is not too mentally demanding to count the number of lengths of the swimming bath you may have covered. But possibly this lack of stimulus can be made up for by the social contacts that can be made by this activity. Swimming is particularly good for people with stiff joints. The buoyancy of the water supports the weight of the body so that movement is made easier.

The only disadvantage (apart from the unpleasant business of getting dry after a swim – but perhaps that is simply a personal reaction) is the distance you may have to travel to your nearest swimming bath.

Dancing, be it ballroom, old-time, country or Scottish, gains maximum points for strength and stamina. Gains in suppleness are restricted mainly to legs, apart from perhaps the more exuberant specialised dancing. Mental agility is a prime necessity in any form of sequence dancing: any lapse of concentration by one participant will bring down the wrath of the rest of the team.

Disadvantages can be lack of local facilities, and possibly lack of a partner. Even if widowhood, or the single status, is not a problem in this direction, both partners may not have similar interests. Men particularly are often resistant to this form of exercise. But the social aspects of an activity that both of you can enjoy may be one way to win him over.

Keep Fit/Aerobics are enjoying much popularity of late. Often the smallest village will have a weekly class. Strength, stamina and suppleness can all be improved by these forms of activity. The advantage of many of the smaller classes is that each activity can be undertaken at your own pace. This becomes increasingly import-ant as you become older – exercise of whatever form should never be undertaken to the point of distress.

Although not mentally demanding, the social contacts made at such classes are valuable. There is nothing quite like the relaxed feeling of wellbeing after an hour's work-out to promote new friendships and cement old ones.

You will usually be able to find a suitable class not too far away from where you live. Disadvantages are that often classes are held in the evenings for the convenience of people who still have to work during the day. For you, now enjoying retirement, the thought of turning out on a wet winter's evening is not too pleasant. Also, classes are usually held on a termly basis (many are run by the local education authority), so for a good part of the year you will have to exercise on your own if you want to keep up some of the benefits gained.

• Elizabeth G. had a sedentary job and, being single with an active mind, had practically every evening filled to capacity with 'things to do and people to see'. But she realised that a daily programme of loosening-up exercises would be of advantage as she reached the middle years.

At the particular time when this aspect of her life was of concern a cassette of the limbering-up exercises of the Paratroop Regiment was available. Elizabeth bought this tape, and each morning bent, stretched and moved to the fiercely barked commands of 'Sergeant'! She found that she never managed to progress any further than the first ten minutes of the tape – the preliminary warm-up before the serious stuff began. Nevertheless, she derived immense benefit from this short period of exercise every morning. (What the neighbours thought is another matter.)

Jogging reached its peak of popularity a few years ago, and it seemed that half the nation were taking to the streets in their track suits. Possibly fewer people are seen out jogging these days, although as the annual marathon runs approach, there is a marked increase in the number of hardy souls in training. Jogging is excellent for improving strength and stamina but, as with walking, only of limited value in improving suppleness, as only the legs are involved in this activity to any degree.

Mental agility will not gain a great deal from jogging. In fact, jogging has been said to be addictive – the very rhythm and inevitability of the next footfall makes it, somehow, a soothing pastime. This, too, can be beneficial.

If you are thinking of taking up jogging for the first time in middle age, do remember to take it slowly at first. Build up gradually to your five – or twenty-five – miles. Too much, too soon, can do damage to unfit muscles and joints as well as putting an unnecessary – and potentially dangerous – strain on your heart. But if you have been a dedicated jogger for a number of years, this may well be the exercise for you.

You will doubtless be able to add many other activities to the list, and the ones mentioned may bring others to your mind.

Exercise scoring table

Activity	Strength	Stamina	Supple-ness	Mental Agility	Possible Problems
Cycling	★	★★	★	★	Danger of accidents
Dancing	★★	★★	★	★★	Lack of suitable facilities
Jogging	★★	★★	★	★	? unsuitable to take up in middle age
Keep Fit	★★	★★	★★	★	Unsuitable times
Rambling	★	★★	★	★	No suitable local walks
Squash/ Tennis	★★	★★	★	★	? too physically demanding
Swimming	★★	★★	★★	★	Distance from local baths

But what about those days when the weather is bitterly cold, snowy or wet, and there is no pleasure at all to be gained from outdoor activity? How can you make sure that all the benefits of regular exercise are not completely lost? A few simple movements practised for ten minutes or so three or four times a week is all that is needed to keep you in trim until conditions improve. The following is a sample selection of exercises that will keep most parts of your body in trim.

Exercises for neck and shoulders:

Sit comfortably on a firm chair with each elbow cupped loosely in the opposite hand. Circle your neck, five times, to its fullest extent, first in a clockwise direction and then, after a brief rest, in an anticlockwise direction.

Still sitting down, with arms held loosely by your sides, hunch both shoulders forward, and then back again five times. Repeat exercise, but hunching shoulders backwards five times. (This exercise is particularly helpful when you are tired after a long drive. With care, it can be done while still at the wheel, if traffic conditions permit.)

Stand with feet comfortably apart. Circle each arm separately, making sure that the circle is as wide as possible each time. (Shoulder joints are the most frequently underused joints in the body. Unless you are a fitness expert, try to remember the last time you stretched your arms fully over your head.)

Exercises for waist and abdomen:

Stand easily with feet slightly apart and raise your arms straight out in front of you. Keeping your hips completely still, swing the top part of your body round to the left as far as possible. Repeat to the right. Do this five times in all, and notice how your waist is stretched and firmed.

Again stand easily with feet slightly apart, hands close to your sides. Slide your left hand as far down the outside of your thigh as you can without leaning forward. Repeat to the right. Again, repeat this sequence five times.

Exercise for hips, knees and toes:

Stand up straight. Mark time on the spot, raising each knee as high as possible each time. (This exercise done to marching music can be almost enjoyable!)

Sit on the floor, legs straight out in front of you and slightly apart. Without leaning on your hands, raise each leg – straight – alternately as far as you are able. Repeat five times. (This sounds easy, but is telling on the thigh and stomach muscles.)

Sit comfortably on a chair. Cross your right leg over your left knee. Circle your ankle five times clockwise, and five times anticlockwise. Repeat with the other leg.

(Remember that sitting with your legs crossed is not normally a good idea. Varicose veins – a relatively common complaint in the middle years – are not helped by this method of sitting. See Appendix.)

This is by no means a complete catalogue of all the ways in which you can keep your body fit by exercise. But the principles are the same whatever the form of exercise. Start today and see the benefits.

SLEEP

There is nothing like daily exercise to help you get a good night's sleep – yet one more good reason for keeping up the exercise in one form or another. If you are truly fit (and are fortunate enough not to suffer from any chronic disease, of course), you will probably sleep well most of the time. And how much better we all feel after a good night's restful sleep. Remember those long, dreamless sleeps of childhood? – either your own, or watching your children when young as they lay peaceful and quiet, fast asleep.

But as we get older, our sleep patterns change. In fact, they change throughout life. Think of the new-born baby who sleeps for around twenty hours out of the twenty-four, and the five-year-olds, most of whom need ten hours or so every night after an energetic day at school. Then, later in life, the few hours that teenagers seem to thrive on when they are active and interested, or, alternatively, the hours and hours they stay in bed when life is uneventful. As routine overtakes us all in the child-rearing and working years the amount of sleep we have is very much dependent on the clock. Only at weekends and holidays do we, at this time of life, get as much sleep as we feel we would like.

Retirement age brings the bonus of no longer being tied to a set routine, and yet how often do we hear of retired people having 'bad nights'. What should you do if sleep is a problem for you?

The first answer is, 'Don't worry about it.' Far more harm is done by lying awake worrying about not sleeping than by not sleeping. Be positive about your problem. Try a few experiments until you find some routine that suits your particular way of life.

1. What time do you go to bed? Are you really tired out by this time? Or is going to bed, for example, at 10 p.m. a habit left over from the days when you had to get up at 7 a.m? If this is the case, try staying up an hour or two longer. Remember that it does not really matter if you sleep an hour longer in the morning now.

2. Do you feel drowsy after lunch? Do you resolutely keep yourself awake at this time, as you had to when you were at work? If so, why? You are more likely to feel energetic and so be able to accomplish more in the afternoon if you have a 'cat-nap' of half an hour or so after lunch. This in turn will ensure that you feel ready for sleep as night approaches. Remember that as well as needing less sleep as you get older, shorter but more frequent periods of sleep may well be beneficial to you.

3. Get into a relaxing bedtime routine. Have a warm, leisurely bath – have a hot, milky drink – read a light, entertaining book before 'lights out'. Herbal teas, for example camomile, can often be beneficial for poor sleepers. Why not try a herb pillow? It may or may not be helpful for you, but you will never know unless you try it.

4. Check on mechanical factors that can affect sleep. Is your bedroom too hot? Is it too cold? A window slightly ajar may be a good idea if your room gets stuffy during the night. Check that there are no creaking doors or radiators, or dripping taps, to awaken you. Are your nightclothes comfortable? Are your bedclothes too heavy? If so, think of changing to a duvet as a lighter, more flexible covering.

5. Try to think about relaxing your muscles, one by one, starting at the tips of your toes. Don't hurry this – work out the function of each muscle and then let it go quite floppy. By the time you have reached your eyelids they are likely to be quietly shut anyway!

If all these manoeuvres fail, and you are wide awake at 3 a.m., with possibly a snoring partner beside you, don't lie there fretting and fuming. Get up and find some – preferably boring – job to do. After a while, the delights of a warm bed will draw you back again – with luck to sleep this time. (Remember to tell your partner that this is what you intend to do if you cannot sleep. Roy and Jeannette found that if one partner went downstairs in the middle of the night, the other automatically thought something was wrong, and came down to see what was the matter. So *two* people were awake for an hour or so for no very good reason.)

Finally, do not forget that sleep may be difficult under certain circumstances. These conditions will need special treatment. Once this has been successfully accomplished, sleep will return again to a normal, healthy pattern.

Depression. People who are clinically depressed (see Chapter 6) show a specific faulty sleep pattern. Waking is early – around 3 or 4 a.m. usually – every morning. And how bleak life can seem during these hours when the vast majority of the world is still asleep. If this is happening to you in addition to feeling low, miserable and lacking in interest during the day, do check with your doctor. Adequate treatment, if you are found to be depressed, will see a welcome return to a normal sleep pattern.

Bereavement. Sleep, along with appetite, is one of the first natural functions to be affected by any bereavement (see Chapter 7), and the closer the tie that has been broken, the worse is the upset in the sleep pattern. Tiredness may be quite overwhelming, but sleep is quite impossible. In these circumstances, ask your doctor for a week's supply of sleeping pills, telling him, of course, of your sleeping problem. This should help you over the very worst of your grief and help to break the pattern of sleepless nights.

Remember, too, that the death of a loved one is not the only bereavement that can happen. Retirement in itself implies a small 'death' of all the ways of life and familiar routines of many years. This is particularly so if retirement or redundancy has been forced on you prematurely. Be gentle with yourself for a while, until you become adjusted to your new situation.

Pain. There is nothing like chronic, niggling pain to wreck a good night's sleep. The pain of arthritis, muscular aches of all kinds or an uncomfortable chest condition will effectively prevent you getting to sleep, and staying asleep. Be sure you are receiving adequate treatment for whatever pain is troublesome. Sleep should then resume a normal, healthy pattern.

Menopausal problems. Sleep can sometimes be a major problem for women during the menopause. 'Hot flushes' can be so frequent and uncomfortable as to render a good night's sleep impossible. Again, formication, that unpleasant feeling of ants running under your skin, can awaken you and prevent you getting back to sleep. Here treatment from your doctor, perhaps in the form of hormone replacement therapy for a short while, will ease the problem. Doctors these days are more sympathetic than they were a decade or so ago about these problems in their female patients, so shop around the doctors in your particular practice until you find one who is responsive to your problems.

We spend, on average, around one-third of our lives in bed, so it is· worth while making this chunk of our lives pleasant – and also worth while from a health point of view. Don't say, 'It's my age.' This may have a small bearing on any problems you may be having, but a little thought can usually sort out most of the causes.

DIET

An important element in anyone's fitness plans. Retirement is a good time to reassess your dietary pattern. But first of all, a few points to remember about food in retirement.

1. It is important to make sure you eat regularly once retirement is upon you. It can be all too easy to skip breakfast, eat a snack lunch and then maybe have a 'convenience' meal in the evening. 'Tomorrow will be different,' you promise yourself. 'I'll cook a proper meal.' But, for a variety of reasons 'tomorrow' never comes.

This state of affairs can occur perhaps more frequently in people who – either by choice or by forced circumstances such as bereavement – live alone. Previous eating patterns also have a bearing on eating routines.

• Dorothy was a career girl all her life. After obtaining her medical degree from one of the prestigious London hospitals, she determined to succeed in her chosen speciality – anaesthetics. A decade later saw Dorothy as a consultant anaesthetist at a large provincial hospital, her ambition fulfilled. But on the way, long and irregular hours of work had taken their toll on her regular pattern of eating.

After a bout of prolonged illness, Dorothy reviewed her current lifestyle and came to the sensible conclusion that from now on she would always eat breakfast, and a good cooked meal in the evening – however difficult this might prove to organise. Her working hours were still about twice as long as average, and she found shopping for food difficult. (Most food stores in those days were shut long before her usual finishing time of 8–9 p.m.)

So Dorothy organised herself to have a large shopping expedition once a month, and always among her purchases were foods that she could make into individual meals and put into the freezer. One half-day a month she set aside to cook and bake 'for the freezer', plating up complete meals that could be taken out and heated quickly in the oven – or, subsequently, in the microwave. In this way, she was sure of being able to get one balanced meal every day.

This pattern stood Dorothy in good stead when the time came for her to retire. (Not that retirement seemed to make much difference to the amount of activity she packed into her day – only the content was different.) There were still the individual meals ready in her freezer for use on a regular daily basis if needed. The only difference was that the meals were more varied and exciting when she found there was more time to shop around for unusual ingredients to use on her cooking days.

For your health's sake it is important that you have one adequately balanced meal every day. Also, why not investigate the possibilities – and much-neglected delights – of a leisurely break-fast now that time is not at such a premium? Perhaps breakfast was distasteful to you during your working life? See how much more pleasant it can be if you take time over a second cup of coffee together with crisp toast or crunchy cereal and a review of yesterday's events in the newspaper.

2. Retirement is *not* the time to try and shed those few extra pounds you have been carrying around for the past decade. Crash slimming diets are definitely not on the agenda. Protein foods are needed daily to replace tissue depleted by normal wear and tear, extra calcium (found in dairy products) is necessary to counteract osteoporosis – the condition which makes the bones of older people brittle and so susceptible to fractures, and a certain amount of carbohydrate is necessary for energy and warmth.

Most of us will have put on weight during the years since we were in our twenties. This, as long as it does not become excessive, is a normal part of the ageing process. One has only to look at a photograph of older members of the family when they were at a similar age to oneself to see the similarity in body shape.

Obviously any tendency to excessive overweight should be guarded against by sensible eating and a reasonable amount of exercise. But don't try to match your weight when you were twenty. You will merely end up looking 'scraggy'!

3. Consider the possibility of having your main meal in the middle of the day, instead of in the evening. During your working life this was, in all probability, inconvenient, if not downright impossible. But now that you have the chance to arrange your life as you wish, it may well be more satisfactory for a number of reasons.

A lighter snack meal in the few hours before bed is certainly better for your digestion.

Food eaten in the middle of the day will have a better chance of being used immediately in energetic activity rather than being stored, for future use, as fat. So this in itself may have a beneficial effect on your weight.

Remember you now have no need to fight off those drowsy feelings that so often assail one after lunch. What is wrong with a post-prandial nap? Many (hot) countries have the right idea and send everyone off for a siesta in the afternoons. (Perhaps if you try this idea, you should go to bed a little later in the evening to avoid night-time waking?)

4. If you are interested in the preparation of food, now is your chance. Perhaps you have nursed a life-long ambition to attend a cordon bleu course? Now is the time to do just this. And to experiment – on your partner or your friends – when you have learned the intricacies of superb food presentation.

5. Remember that as we get older digestive systems, in many people, become less efficient. Foods that hitherto you were able to eat with impunity now give rise to unpleasant attacks of indigestion. It is no good fighting against this, or trying to ignore it altogether. Accept it and enjoy only those particular foods which do not disagree with you.

By the time you have reached retirement, you are probably aware of the constituents of a good diet. But perhaps a word or two to refresh your memory will not come amiss.

Food consists of three main ingredients, protein, carbohydrates and fats, together with important extras in the form of vitamins and minerals. It is the blending together of these constituents in the correct proportions, with the addition of fibre or 'roughage', that makes for a healthy, balanced diet.

Protein. These foods, built up from a number of substances known as amino-acids, are the building bricks of the body. All cells of the body need protein for growth and repair. Obviously in the retirement age group, protein is no longer needed for growth, but a certain daily amount is very necessary for maintenance and repair of all the tissues of the body.

First-class protein is found in meat, eggs, cheese and fish. Nuts, leguminous vegetables and milk are all good sources of second-class protein. Generally speaking a greater amount of food containing only second-class protein needs to be eaten to obtain sufficient for daily needs, but an entirely vegetarian diet, relying completely on second-class protein, can be quite satisfactory. (Do not forget the advantages of 'a pint of milk a day' – in whatever form you wish. Milk is an excellent source of calcium, which is necessary for healthy bones during the middle years.)

Carbohydrates. These are the starchy, sweet foods, and are the ones that should be eaten with caution to avoid excess weight gain. Carbohydrates should by no means be reduced too drastically in your diet, but do not go overboard on sticky pastries and sweets. Avoid two or three heaped teaspoonfuls of sugar in your tea or coffee: if you really cannot stand these drinks unsweetened, try artificial sweeteners.

Bread and potatoes are valuable sources of energy and warmth, so do not avoid them altogether. Wholemeal bread, and potatoes baked in their jackets, are excellent sources of fibre as well as of certain vitamins and minerals.

Fat. Much has been written about the benefits of unsaturated fats in the prevention of heart attacks. But if you really do feel deprived without your portion of butter at breakfast time, this small amount will cause you no problem. It is as well to avoid excesses of fatty meat, and scones and teacakes piled high with butter should also be left for the occasional treat.

Fats are a necessary component of the daily diet, but – as with everything – should be enjoyed in moderation.

Vitamins and minerals. Small amounts of these substances are widely distributed in different foods, and are vital to health. A good mixed diet will contain all the vitamins and minerals necessary for health, so there is no need to swallow extra vitamin pills. Remember to eat, however, at least two portions of fruit every day (preferably at least one portion of one of the citrus fruits) to supply the body's need for vitamin C. This vitamin cannot be stored in the body, so an adequate daily intake is necessary.

Two or three portions of fruit – of any sort – will also help to provide adequate fibre and roughage.

Fibre and roughage. With our comparatively refined diet today, our bowels are deprived of adequate bulk for healthy peristalsis – the movement of the bowel which pushes food through the yards of intestine. Without this active movement, constipation is an all too frequent fact of life. This in turn can lead to other problems in the large bowel.

Your aim should be to eat regularly and adequately. Enjoy what you eat, but try to avoid excess of any one group of food such as, for example, large quantities of sticky buns or cream cakes. In other words, everything in moderation!

This applies also to your alcohol intake. The pattern of your drinking – or non-drinking – will, by retirement age, be well established, and just because you have reached a certain time in your life, there is no good reason to alter this. Unless, of course, you have a drink problem. If this is the case, what better time to get help and kill it, once and for all, than now – when your whole life is on the change?

But for those people who enjoy a glass of wine with their meal, a glass of sherry or a pint or two of beer in the evening, why not continue to enjoy this relaxation? There is good medical evidence to show that a small daily amount of alcohol actually protects against coronary heart disease. A recent piece of research shows that teetotal men show a slightly higher incidence of heart disease than do those men who drink a little alcohol. Too much alcohol obviously has adverse physical effects, as well as leading to much social and financial distress. Again the keyword is moderation.

These then are the routine daily ways in which you can ensure that you keep your body in as good a working order as possible. At first sight it may seem a formidable list. But when you come to analyse the different elements you will realise that much is what you do regularly and automatically anyway.

5 · Body maintenance

As well as keeping up good habits of exercise, diet and so on to ensure fitness, you should establish a routine of checking on various aspects of body function to make sure that you get the utmost from your retirement years. This is what I mean by 'body maintenance'. The areas that you should aim to check on, at regular intervals, are listed alphabetically for ease of reference, not in order of importance.

BLOOD PRESSURE

Everyone has heard of blood pressure. 'He's got blood pressure, you know,' is often the quiet remark heard about someone who is ill. In fact, he would be very ill indeed if he hadn't 'got blood pressure'.

The average normal blood pressure in a young, healthy adult is 120/80 mm mercury. As we mature this pressure rises, owing to many factors, the decreased elasticity of the walls of the blood vessels being just one of these. So at retirement age, a reading of around 140–150/85–90 mms mercury is quite likely in a healthy person.

These readings are only one guide to the health of the heart and circulatory system. There is much else that must be taken into consideration – any symptom you may be having, the sounds of the heart and lungs and the reading from an electro-cardiogram, for example. The control of the blood pressure is a highly complex matter and involves a number of other bodily systems as well as the heart and blood vessels. Strokes and heart attacks have a close relationship with higher blood pressure.

Many medical practices in Britain run blood pressure clinics where all patients over a certain age have regular blood pressure measurements. (A recent Medical Research Council trial into medication and raised blood pressure has just finished a large study which correlated work from general practices all over the country.) Other practices rely on a routine blood pressure check for everyone over a certain age when they attend the surgery for some other condition. If your blood pressure is found to be significantly raised over several readings your doctor will probably advise treatment.

Checking blood pressure is not a facet of body maintenance that you can readily do yourself. There are do-it-yourself blood pressure measurement machines on the market, probably not an entirely good idea: why not let the experts make the test and then interpret the result together with other aspects of your health?

BREASTS

This important aspect of body maintenance applies only to women. (Men can have breast lumps, but this is rare.)

There are many conditions affecting the breast other than cancer, but it is this condition that is most feared, and indeed that must be diagnosed and treated as early as possible. However, it is unwise to lose all sense of proportion over the issue and think that every lump found in the breast is necessarily cancerous. A few facts and figures will put the situation in perspective.

Around 80 per cent of all breast lumps are due to causes other than cancer.

Only around 8–10 per cent of all women will suffer from breast cancer.

The majority of breast cancers occur in older women. These cancers tend to be slow growing in about 50 per cent of cases. So, with early treatment, the chances of many trouble-free years are high.

On the negative side, it must be remembered that:

About 30 per cent of all cancers in women are cancers of the breast.

About 15,000 women die as a result of breast cancer in Britain every year.

But remember two further facts:

Many of these women will be well advanced in years.

Double this number will die from other conditions, infections such as pneumonia for example. (Quoted from *What Every-woman Should Know about her Breasts* by Patricia Gilbert, Sheldon Press, 1986.)

But figures and statistics never seem particularly relevant when one is considering one's own body. So what should you be doing to ensure that any breast condition you may be suffering from will be found and treated early?

Remember that you will be the first person to discover the smallest lump in your breast. However efficient are methods of screening for breast lumps (mammography, for example), there must of necessity be a long gap between examinations, whereas – living intimately with your breasts as you do – you will be able to find the tiniest lump as soon as it is capable of being felt if you organise yourself into a routine to examine your breasts regularly. And it is important that you do this examination properly.

SELF-EXAMINATION OF BREASTS

1. The timing should be every month. If you are still men-struating, set your examination time for just after a period: if you do the examination just before a period is due, you may well find all sorts of lumps and bumps. Many women's breasts do become somewhat lumpy, quite normally, immediately before a period.

2. Be sure you have adequate time to perform the examination. There is no point in checking for lumps if you are going to hurry: in this way tiny lumps are missed. Take the telephone off the hook – let the doorbell ring. If it is that important the caller will try again. You will only need about ten minutes to do an adequate examination.

3. Method of examination.
   Strip to the waist and sit in front of a mirror.

Look at both breasts, and note:

if they are any 'different' from usual;

if there is any obvious irregularity;

if there is any discharge from the nipple;

if the nipple is being pulled to one side.

Then put your hands behind your head, and repeat.

Lie on your back on your bed, with a pillow under the shoulder of the same side as the breast you are going to examine. (This will push your breast forward so that examination can be more thorough.)

With the flat of your fingers feel – gently but firmly – your breast. Start around the nipple and work round and outwards in a circular fashion until you have covered the whole of your breast. If you conscientiously pursue this method, you will be sure that you have felt every part of your breast. Finally, move your fingers up into your armpit. The breast tissue extends into this region rather like a tail. It is important not to miss this part of your breast.

Move the pillow under the other shoulder and repeat the procedure on the other breast.

Finally, check for swellings in each armpit, and also in the little hollow above your collarbone.

A tedious procedure maybe, but one that is well worth taking time over.

The next question, of course, is what to do if you do find a lump in one of your breasts.

First of all, DON'T PANIC! Remember that just because you have felt a lump, this does not automatically mean that it is cancerous. There are a number of other conditions of the breast – fibro-cystic disease, lipomas, cysts etc. – that are very common.

The second thing to do is to make an appointment to see your doctor – within the week. No need to demand an appointment that very day, but it is advisable to get your particular lump checked as soon as possible. Your doctor will then be able to advise you as to what further steps are necessary, depending on his diagnosis of your lump.

Many surgeries and health centres have screening programmes for all kinds of conditions. (A screening programme is one that checks a whole population for one specific condition.) Mammography is checking for lumps in the breast by X-ray examination. This method is not used widely to check every woman at present, but rather as a tool when once a lump has been discovered to find out more about the type of swelling present. But don't forget that this test can be performed, at most, only once a year. You will be able to examine your breasts far more regularly than this.

Breast self-examination is an important part of body maintenance for all women – particularly those in the retirement age group. Do not lose out on the chances of early treatment by neglecting this aspect of health care.

FEET

In Britain, chiropody is free on the National Health Service for everyone over the age of sixty. Facilities differ in different parts of the country. In some towns there are long waiting lists, in others senior citizens' feet can be checked every three months or so. Naturally, if you are able quite easily to keep your own feet in good trim you will not need the services of a chiropodist, but the service is available if you need it. Enquire at your local Community Health Offices, your own general practitioner or the Citizens Advice Bureau for local facilities. Alternatively check the Yellow Pages of the telephone directory for private chiropodists. These specialists in foot-care work from:

National Health Service premises;

a health centre;

their own premises.

A home-visiting service is available for special conditions where people are unable to get out and about;

visits to old people's homes or retirement homes are also sometimes, and in some places, available.

It is vitally important that your feet should be comfortable.

Painful feet, whether due to an arthritic condition or merely to corns or callouses, are a potent factor in reduced mobility, which becomes increasingly important as one ages.

To check on a few simple ways to look after your feet.

1. Wear comfortable, well-fitting shoes. Men are better at looking after themselves in this respect than are women. Some fashion shoes spell disaster to feet, so wear them to look good only on special occasions and for everyday wear be sure that you buy really well-fitting shoes. Slippers too should be of the firm well-fitting kind. Worn-down, soft, floppy slippers – however much you may be attached to them – will do nothing at all for your feet.

2. Keep your feet warm in winter. Thicker stockings or tights for women together with fur-lined boots for the worst of the winter months is a sensible precaution. Socks should be of a wool mixture. Socks made of nylon do little to keep feet warm in winter and are best avoided at any time of the year as they tend to become dampened very easily by perspiration. In very cold weather why not invest in some of the long, cosy thermal underwear? If your legs are warm the chances are that your feet, too, will not feel the cold.

3. Circulation needs to be kept going in the legs and feet as we mature, and especially so in cold weather.

A few simple foot exercises (see Chapter 4), as well as increasing mobility of the feet, will improve the circulation.

Put your feet up if you are sitting still for any length of time. In this way the blood will be able more readily to return to the heart to be pumped round the body again. Perhaps now is the time to start thinking about treating yourself to a reclining chair? Alternatively – and a good deal cheaper – is a simple footstool.

Remember not to wear tight garters to hold up socks or stockings. These can impede the smooth flow of blood in the legs. Varicose veins are also not helped by anything tight around the legs.

Keep your toenails in trim by cutting them straight across to avoid ingrowing toenails. Rub handcream or oil into your feet after a bath to help prevent hard skin from forming on heels and around toenails. This is particularly important if you have a tendency to a dry skin.

There are a few specific conditions to be aware of as you consider your foot care:

1. *Corns and callouses* – unless very minor – should be treated professionally by a chiropodist. On no account cut your own corns. Apart from being a somewhat painful procedure, you may end up with a nasty foot infection unless you are extremely careful. If this should happen to you, do get your doctor's advice quickly so as to prevent further – possibly more serious – trouble.

2. *Injuries* to feet (and this includes those mentioned above if you do attempt your own pedicure) should receive prompt attention from your doctor if you are in any doubt at all about the speed at which healing is taking place. As we get older, the blood supply to our extremities is less efficient. Any minor abrasion or other injury will therefore take longer to heal than if sustained during the twenties or thirties.

3. If you are *diabetic* you must take especial care of your feet. You will be automatically on the priority list for chiropody care. If you are finding this difficult to obtain, check with your doctor. Part of the problem associated with diabetes is an inefficient blood supply particularly to the feet, so extra special care must be taken to prevent injury.

4. *Chilblains* can be the bane of some people's lives. These itchy, red, swollen areas on toes or heels can make walking a misery, and when warm in bed can itch abominably. Prevention is by keeping feet cosy, warm and dry in cold and damp weather. Keeping the circulation going is also of importance. But some people, in spite of all their efforts, do seem particularly prone to ·chilblains. Treatment is difficult, and everyone has their own favourite remedies – from painting the chilblains with iodine to bathing them alternately in hot and then cold water. Avoid direct heat on chilblains. Toasting them in front of a fire or on a hot water bottle will only make them worse. Fortunately, chilblains are a

self-limiting condition, and will improve with the onset of warmer weather.

5. Again, *ingrowing toenails* are a condition with which you may have been familiar all your life. By the time retirement comes you will be aware of the steps you need to take to stop, as far as possible, problems in this direction. Broad guidelines include:

Shoes and socks should be large enough to prevent undue pressure on toenails.

Careful cutting of toenails, straight across.

Some sufferers also find a small 'pack' of cotton-wool under the affected nail is beneficial.

If this aspect of your foot care is deteriorating, check with your doctor.

Feet stand a good deal of wear and tear throughout a long life. By the time retirement age is reached, the number of steps your feet have taken must be almost uncountable. So be sure to look after those faithful extremities and they will continue to serve you well for many years to come.

HEARING

The numerous advertisements in daily newspapers about aids for the 'hard of hearing' seem to imply that there is a universal panacea for hearing loss in the middle years. In reality there are very many reasons why hearing can be less than perfect as middle age is reached.

As we mature, the delicate structures of the ear become less mobile and so, in practically everyone, hearing is reduced to a greater or lesser extent as the years go by. But quite apart from this, there are two main causes of more severe forms of deafness that can afflict people.

1. *Conductive deafness.* This is the deafness which occurs when some part of the auditory apparatus becomes blocked or damaged by disease. Probably one of the commonest forms of this

type of deafness in the middle years is the build-up of wax in the outer ear. This is where your scheme of body maintenance can be of value. If you find you are getting somewhat deaf – your friends and family will probably be as much aware of this as you are – check with your doctor. If you do have excess wax blocking the way in for the sound waves, a simple syringing will soon clear the problem. (Whatever you do, do not poke your ears with any object. Damage to the delicate lining of the ear canal at best, or to the eardrum at worst, can be the result of this practice.)

There are, of course, other conditions that can give rise to a conductive deafness. From the body maintenance point of view, there is little that you can do personally, apart from obtaining your doctor's help and advice.

2. *Sensori-neural deafness* is the type of hearing loss that occurs when the inner ear together with its nerve supply has been damaged. Infection by certain viruses can be a cause of this – mumps in childhood, for example. Again there is little you can do to minimize this, apart from getting medical help.

Many people reaching middle age have problems with their hearing to some degree or other. Do not attempt to deny this fact if it should happen to you. Seek medical advice. There is a good chance that the condition can be improved. And do remember that once your friends realise that you are a little hard of hearing, they will be sympathetic. It is when they are unaware that you have a problem in this direction that they can become irritated when you do not quite catch on to what they are trying to say to you. Simple ways of helping you will come naturally to them if they recognise your problem. Speaking more slowly will help, as will also facing you directly when they are speaking. It is amazing how many clues we unknowingly pick up by the expression on people's faces and the movement of their mouths. These clues become of far greater importance if your hearing should be diminishing over the years. Blindness is apparent to everyone; deafness is not, and so can be far more damaging to social contacts.

SKIN

The condition of the skin as we get older is probably more a female concern than a masculine one: nevertheless, similar changes take place in the skin of both sexes. These are modified to some extent in women by the care – or otherwise – taken of the skin throughout life. Wrinkles affect us all, and are often taken as a measure of age. (In fact, current youth slang uses the unkind term 'wrinklies' for all people over about fifty.)

These signs of ageing are caused by a number of quite normal physiological changes in the skin, most importantly the loss of subcutaneous fat and of elastic tissue. Heredity also plays a part. We inherit our skin type – be it greasy or dry – along with other physical characteristics, from our parents: if yours had early wrinkling of their skin, the chances are high that you will also. Dry skins tend to wrinkle more, and earlier, than do greasy skins.

This last fact indicates the steps that you can take to minimise ageing in the skin.

1. Probably the single most important thing to do is to keep the skin moist – in other words to prevent it becoming dehydrated. There are a multitude of products on the market to counteract the drying of the skin – some expensive and some relatively cheap. Moisturising creams do not need to be expensive to be effective: the regularity with which they are used is the important factor. Moisturise your face every night before bed, after thoroughly cleansing the skin by whatever means you normally use. Remember not to rub your face dry. Pat it almost dry, and then leave a film of moisture to dry naturally, letting this absorb slowly before you apply your night cream. Always wear a moisturising cream under make-up.

2. Still on the 'anti-dehydration' theme – sunbathing is not popular with dry skins. Excessive sunbathing in younger days may well show up as wrinkles during the middle years. Always – *always* – wear a sunscreen cream with a suitable screening factor for your

type of skin. (Our great-grandmothers certainly knew what they were about, by way of preventing wrinkles, when they sat under their parasols.)

3. Smoking, as well as having deleterious effects on many aspects of health, does no good for wrinkles either. Along with the drying of the skin of the face goes the specific effect of the drug on the blood vessels.

4. Excess alcohol (by no means does this implicate the occasional social drink) can also lead to tiny broken veins which mar the surface of the skin.

5. If you live in a centrally-heated house, the atmosphere can become very dry. Open fires, or a window slightly ajar, will help with this to some extent. But it is worth thinking about a humidifier of some kind (a saucer of water is one of the simplest, and cheapest, of humidifiers) to prevent the air becoming dry. Skin can also react to this form of dryness.

6. The exposed skin of the face should always be protected against cold winds as well as excess sunlight. Here again, a moisturising cream will be of great value.

7. Finally, do check on the type of make-up that you use now that you are in the middle years. The colour and texture that suited you admirably a decade or so ago are not likely to do much for your appearance now. It is worth getting some good beauty advice so that you can purchase suitable types and shades of make-up from now on. (Do remember to go lightly on the face powder. There is nothing more ageing than a network of fine wrinkles clogged with excess powder.)

Then, those brown spots that appear – almost overnight it seems – on the exposed parts of your body: backs of hands, faces and upper arms particularly. These patches of irregular pigmentation would seem in some way to be connected with exposure of the skin to the sun. There is little that can be done either to prevent them or to limit them once they have appeared. The most you can do, if you really are concerned about their appearance, is to camouflage them with make-up, but even this can be difficult, as it will have to be reapplied each time you wash your hands. Perhaps it is best to just accept them. These marks are in no way dangerous.

Other moles or raised areas on the skin must be watched carefully, however. If one of these marks

starts growing quickly;

bleeds, or becomes red and sore;

becomes very much darker and more raised;

you should ask your doctor to have a look at it. Occasionally these moles, which have probably been present all your life, can become malignant. Early treatment effects a complete cure. Watch also particularly any moles or raised areas around the 'mask' area of the face. These can become locally malignant and are known as 'rodent ulcers'. Excision by a skilled surgeon will remove them with very little trace.

One further problem that can affect your skin is irritation. This is often associated with dry skins and moisturisers will help. Soaking in a hot bath can often bring on this irritation, so shorten the time you lie in the bath, or think about having a shower instead. Be careful, also, of the type of soap you use. Highly perfumed varieties can sometimes lead to an allergic skin rash which itches abominably.

A condition known as 'intertrigo' can affect skin in those parts of the body that are warm and moist, for example, the armpits, groin and, in women with heavy breasts, beneath the breasts. The skin becomes red and sore and can, if not treated, be made even worse by an added fungal infection. Preventive measures include:

careful and frequent washing of these parts of the body;

extra care when drying the skin here;

a *light* dusting of talcum powder will also help, but go easy on this – too much will clog the skin even further;

be sure that clothes are loose-fitting so that adequate ventilation of those areas can occur. For example, stockings instead of tights – loose-fitting underpants for men – cotton and wool mixture shirts and blouses, rather than nylon which holds in the moisture.

✻   ✻   ✻

Our skins show to the outside world how we are ageing. Be sure your skin ages as well as possible, and that the inevitable wrinkles are happy ones.

TEETH

Besides enhancing our appearance, teeth are important for proper mastication of food. Teeth also play a role in speech. As any speech therapist will tell you, good and correct contact between teeth and tongue is important in the production of good, clear speech.

For all these reasons it is important that during the middle years teeth should be looked after as carefully as you looked after your children's teeth when they were small. Regular visits to the dentist are still necessary. The conditions in the mouth that your dentist will be treating are now different maybe, but, nevertheless, attention is still necessary.

Dental caries is fortunately less during the middle years – this painful condition reaches a peak in the twenties and thirties – but gum disease becomes more of a problem. Gums recede leaving more of the teeth on view (the origin of the expression 'long in the tooth').

Along with this can go infection unless you are meticulous in your daily mouth care. Regular visits to the dentist for de-scaling of the plaque you have been unable to remove by brushing is a necessary adjunct to your own efforts.

Fillings in teeth can become loose and maybe even fall out. This will also need the attention of your dentist if you are not to lose the tooth altogether. Fortunately these days there is much that can be done to avoid dentures by the fitting of crowns and bridges. This can be a lengthy procedure if your mouth is in a bad state of repair, but well worth doing for the final effect.

Dentures, too, do not last for ever, and, indeed, can become loose and ill-fitting as the musculature around the mouth alters. It is very ageing – as well as giving difficulties with eating – to have poorly fitting dentures. Dentures these days are vastly better than our grandparents had to wear – if indeed they had any to wear at all. Do not be too distressed if you have to resign yourself to dentures. They could do much for your appearance once you have got used to them. Remember that you will be joining the 50 per cent of people in the western world who have lost all their teeth by the time they have reached their sixtieth birthday.

Closely allied to the care of teeth are the changes that occur with the sensation of taste. Mouths become drier as less saliva is secreted, and bad breath can become a problem. To avoid this, take especial care when cleaning gums and teeth. A mouthwash can also be refreshing. A well-balanced diet, with an adequate intake of vitamins, will also help. Vitamin A, concerned as it is with the repair of mucous membranes such as that lining the mouth, is especially important in this context. This vitamin is found in dairy produce, liver, fish and green vegetables.

Remember, too, that as you get older taste will alter. The sense of smell is closely allied to taste, and, after the age of sixty or so, you may not be able to savour food as much as you did when you were younger. You may well find that you are increasing the amount of seasoning you put into the cooking to an excessive degree, maybe so much that younger relatives find your meals too spicy and salty. Extra salt is not good for your health generally. So be aware of this as you season your cooking or add extra salt at the table.

Finally, any ulcer or sore in your mouth which does not heal quickly should receive the attention of your doctor. Everyone gets the occasional mouth ulcer, but if this has not cleared up in two or three weeks, get advice.

VISION

Anyone who reaches retirement age without needing spectacles is lucky. Whether you have to wear them all the time, or carry them around with you to read labels and prices in the supermarket, it is most unlikely that you will be able to manage without them altogether.

Checking on the continuing suitability of your spectacles is one of the vital items of body maintenance. Vision is one of the most important ways in which information about the surrounding world is received. Any deterioration in this form of sensory input can lead to social isolation and a host of other problems.

The commonest condition as regards sight that comes with maturity is difficulty in seeing nearby objects clearly. Distance vision is good, and you will be able to see the tiniest speck of a bird or high-flying aircraft in the sky as well as ever you could, but when it comes to reading the telephone directory it is a different matter altogether. You will wish your arms were about twice as long so that you could hold the book far enough away to be able to see clearly. This condition is known as 'presbyopia'. The reason behind this phenomenon is that with age the lens of the eye becomes less able to adapt its shape to view objects at different distances. Glasses specifically designed to your own requirements will overcome this problem. For people who normally have to wear glasses continuously for other reasons, bifocals or the newer variable lenses will remove the need to carry around – and lose – two pairs of glasses. The prescription for your glasses should be checked, and maybe changed, every two or three years, so it is important to visit your optician at regular intervals.

Colours also become less sharp as we age, and adaptation to darkness will also take longer. So remember to take these factors into consideration as you choose clothes or furnishings, or when you go out at night.

People who have worn spectacles for short-sightedness through-out their lives will have an advantage, in some ways, over the long-sighted. Often they will find they need to take their glasses *off* to read. Difficulties can result under these circumstances if contact lenses are worn: glasses will then be needed to 'correct the correction' and so make reading possible.

But whatever type of visual aids you may have to wear, do be sure that you have them checked regularly by your optician. He will also be able to advise you if there is any further, more serious, condition affecting your eyes, in which case he will refer you either to your own doctor or to the local hospital ophthalmic department. (See Appendix for conditions affecting the eye.)

Adequate and suitably placed lights are of great assistance for comfortable reading and close work. Many and varied types of table and reading lamps are available for purchase, including the expensive but very useful magnifying lights. These are to be found in sewing and knitting shops, primarily for use with tapestry work, but they can be adapted for many purposes. Do not think it is 'elderly' to use one of these lamps.

• Jean was a great enthusiast for all aspects of handicraft in any spare time she had from her demanding full-time job. But the time came, when she was in her early fifties, that she had to restrict certain of her craft activities to the daylight hours because she was unable to see to do fine work by artificial light.

Her husband had offered to buy her a magnifying light for her fiftieth birthday, but Jean politely refused, saying that it really would be admitting to ageing. 'Perhaps on my sixtieth birthday, please John,' she said firmly.

So on the morning of her sixtieth birthday a large square box was delivered. On opening it she found a magnifying light complete with a good solid base and adjustable arm suitable for swinging over the arm of a chair. Jean was quite delighted with this, and now says she cannot imagine how she managed all those years without it.

Similarly, do not dismiss the use of a small magnifying lens. It is far better to have one readily available in a pocket than to get on the wrong underground train because you cannot see the map in the back of your diary.

WEIGHT

Weight can become a problem in the middle years for some people. Whether you are someone who puts on weight as soon as you look at a cream cake, or one of those fortunates who can eat anything and not put on an ounce is very dependent on your family history. Fat parents tend to have fat children – and this continues throughout life. It is difficult to decide how much excess weight is determined by a 'natural' tendency and how much by the type of eating pattern set by the family, but there is an undoubted family pattern: some families 'burn up' their food at a greater rate than others.

Whichever category you fall into, you will be aware of it by the time you reach middle age. And at this stage you will have realised, too, that there is not too much you can do about your basic inheritance.

Too much excess weight can cause health problems, and it is advisable to try not to put on too much weight. If you follow the advice regarding exercise and diet in Chapter 4 it is unlikely that you will be too much overweight. It is unwise to attempt to become too slim at this time of your life. Besides not looking particularly attractive, it is all too easy to miss out on a number of vital nutrients if you diet too rigorously. For example, if you virtually cut out all dairy products, you will be denying yourself the calcium which is of such importance to healthy bones in the middle years.

What is a satisfactory weight? Obviously there is a wide variation in ideal weight, dependent on height and build. For example, it is quite satisfactory for a 5 foot 10 inch, 55-year-old man of large build to weigh 13 stones, but the same weight in a 55-year-old woman of five feet tall and with a slight build would be quite unsuitable. A good rule of thumb to determine a suitable weight for you personally is to remember how much you weighed on your twenty-first birthday, or on your wedding day, for example. Add one stone to this weight if you are between 50 and 60 years of age, and you won't be far off your ideal weight. (Exceptions will, of course, always prove the rule. If you weighed 20 stone on your wedding day, these calculations will not be for you. You un-doubtedly have a weight problem – and always have had.)

Be sensible about weight – do not let dieting become a fetish.

Adapt to a slightly larger waistline: if you are too thin in the middle years, you will tend to look older than you really are.

Perhaps this is a good point at which to mention – very briefly – smoking. Many ex-smokers have found that when they gave up smoking they put on a good deal of weight. (The one thing not to do under these circumstances is to start smoking again.) Two reasons are possible for this. Food tastes better when not overlaid with an aura of nicotine, and perhaps sweets were used in the early stages as a substitute.

Smoking can do damage to both health and fitness. Everyone must be aware now of the conclusive medical evidence on the relationship of heart and lung disease to smoking. For this reason alone, giving up smoking – if you have not already done so – should be one of your retirement resolutions. But general fitness, the ability to walk without distress up a hill for example, are also much reduced if you smoke.

Finally, think of the money you will save if you do not smoke – enough for an extra weekend break a year.

WHEN TO CONTACT THE DOCTOR

By the time middle age is reached everyone is aware of how to deal with minor episodes of illness in themselves and their immediate family. For example, a common cold needs rest, plenty of fluids and aspirin or Paracetamol for headache. After two or three days the worst of the symptoms are over and you will be on the road to recovery. Similarly, a mild dose of diarrhoea and vomiting – be it due to something that you have eaten or to 'something that is going the rounds' – can be treated by fluids only, rest and a dose or two of a kaolin and morphia mixture from any chemist.

But there are certain danger signs which should always lead you to seek the advice of your doctor.

1. Unusual bleeding from anywhere in your body. This includes bleeding from the bowel (in vomiting or from the lower

bowel); from any skin lesion such as a mole; from the urinary tract; or being coughed up from the lungs. This particular symptom relating to any system of the body needs immediate investigation.

2. Any sudden pain in the chest. Even if this is associated with a current chest infection such as a cold or the 'flu, you should check with your doctor. He will then be able to exclude any further problems in either your heart or lungs.

3. Any sudden onset of breathlessness. Again this may be in association with a chest infection, but other more serious causes must be excluded.

4. Any persistent symptoms of indigestion. Everyone suffers from indigestion at some time or other, but if this happens to you with greater frequency than is usual for you, your doctor will need to check on heart function as well as looking for any signs of stomach problems.

5. Any change in bowel habit. For example, if your bowels have been regular all your life, and you now find you are suffering from alternate constipation and diarrhoea, contact your doctor for his advice and diagnosis.

6. Persistent headache. The cause may be migraine or some current infection, but if the character of the headache is different from that which is usual for you, it is advisable to check on this with your doctor.

7. Persistent pains in joints which are not helped by routine painkillers, and which keep you awake at night should be referred to your doctor for help.

8. Any lump or swelling anywhere in your body must receive your doctor's advice. He will then be able to refer you for further advice and treatment if he thinks this is necessary.

If you are sure to obtain your doctor's advice on any of the above symptoms, there will be little chance of any serious condition being missed. Remember, any doctor would far rather reassure you on the non-serious nature of your condition than that you should fail to ask his advice about something that may be serious.

✳   ✳   ✳

As we get older there are certain medical conditions from which we are more likely to suffer than we did in our younger days. The infectious diseases, such as measles and mumps, are a thing of the past. (Having said that, one of my first visits as a young GP was to an elderly couple – well into their seventies – who had chickenpox. Which only goes to show that *anything* is possible in medicine.)

Very generally speaking, the medical problems that can afflict us all can be divided into four main classifications:

1. Congenital conditions – those problems which some babies are born with, as, for example, cleft palate.

2. The infectious diseases ranging from whooping cough to herpes.

3. The degenerative diseases. These are the conditions which can arise after a lifetime of 'wear and tear' in our tissues.

4. The growths or tumours. These range from the benign fatty lumps (known as lipomas) through the slow-growing and only locally malignant growths, such as rodent ulcers, to the frankly malignant – and potentially life-threatening – cancers, such as cancer of the lung, breast or bowel.

At retirement age, any congenital problems have either been dealt with years ago, or else we have learned to live with them. The infectious diseases of childhood are behind us (with rare exceptions), and we have built up some immunity to the more common of the infections around us. This does not mean to say that you will never suffer from colds, 'flu, bronchitis etc. once you are over the age of sixty, but the frequent infections of childhood – and sometimes of early middle life when there are young children in the home – will be a thing of the past. It is still important, however, to take advantage of any recommended immunisations against specific diseases if you should be travelling to faraway locations. Your travel agent, or general practitioner, will advise you on this.

It is the two last categories of conditions that account for most of the ill-health in the retirement age group. Infection can also play a part in bodies weakened by any one of the diseases in these two categories. The Appendix on pp. 148–180 lists some of the conditions which tend to affect people in later life and is intended to be used in conjunction with the advice and information given by your doctor.

6 · *Lifestyle*

Good health is much dependent on mental attitudes: the power of the mind over the body really is very great, and stress (or 'mental distress') has been postulated as a significant factor in the onset of many diseases – heart attacks, colds, ulcerative colitis, rheumatoid arthritis, to mention just a few. While this is obviously not the whole story, the way we approach each new situation does affect health.

At retirement a whole new lifestyle opens up, and it would be a foolish person who denied that the necessary adaptation has far-reaching psychological implications. The whole question of relationships with other people, as well as other psychological aspects, is very much involved with this adaptive process. Get these relationships right, and you have a firm foundation on which to build a positive retirement – with a high chance of good health as a spin-off.

These aspects, together with financial and leisure advice, are well covered in the many excellent pre-retirement courses that are becoming increasingly available. Many firms arrange for their employees who are approaching retirement to attend one of these courses. If you have not had the chance to attend one, information can be obtained on what is available in your locality from the Pre-Retirement Association, 19 Undine Street, London SW17 8PP, telephone 01-767 3225. The magazine *Choice* has many interesting articles, as well as information on holidays, courses and so on. This is available from newsagents, or by paying an annual subscription (at present £12.50) to Choice, Subscription Department, 12 Bedford Row, London WC1R 4DX, telephone 01-404 4320. Even if you have recently already retired there is absolutely no reason why you should not still attend a pre-retirement course.

A brief look at some of the specific relationship changes that occur at retirement will help to focus your thinking on retirement lifestyle.

RELATIONSHIP WITH PEERS

This is the area where the greatest change will be noticed. No longer will you be part of the work team. As the run-up to retirement accelerates you will probably feel that someone else is taking over *your* job. This is, of course, true, and it requires a definite act of will not to resent it, and to resist saying, 'I have always done so-and-so this way.' Remember your successor is bound to change the way the job is done as soon as you have left. It is important to try and cultivate a positive attitude during those last few – perhaps difficult – months at work. Look forward to your new life and what you intend to do rather than remaining immersed in your job as you probably have been for most of your life.

Personality plays a large part in the way in which these changes are approached, as does how deeply you were involved with your job. Men and women who put every minute of every day into their work will probably find the transition to retirement more difficult than people who have other hobbies and interests. It is too late at retirement to change one's personality, but acknowledging the problem is half-way to overcoming any difficulties in adjustment.

For some people the loss of status at not being a breadwinner can be a very hard state with which to come to terms. It seems that no one any longer needs your advice or help, and this can come hard if it was formerly you to whom everyone turned to sort out their problems. But remember the world is full of problems, and there are many niches into which your skills in this direction will be welcomed. What about investigating the possibility of becoming involved with local government, one of the major charities or – if you have skills in this direction – part-time teaching at one of your local adult education centres? Perhaps one of your leisure interests will provide an outlet – an amateur musician is always welcome to help youngsters with the rudiments of music, and a skilled carpenter is worth his weight in gold to the local amateur dramatic society, for example. As you become more involved in such activities, you will regain at least some of your status – in your own eyes especially. Everyone needs to be needed. In retirement you must be sure that people around you know that you are willing and able to lend a hand with your particular skills.

Alongside this aspect may come the realisation that you still have many unfulfilled ambitions in relation to your work. Many people in their early working lives set their sights on where they would like to be at around retirement age, a goal which probably few reach. While you are still working there always seems the possibility that you will, after all, fulfil your ambition, but when retirement is a fact, or is even vaguely on the horizon, it begins to come home that this will not be so.

This is the time when you must do some active positive thinking. Think over all the achievements of your working life. Set these alongside the problems you have had to overcome – the illness of a close member of the family or closing down of your place of work, for example. Then, bearing in mind all the difficulties that have been overcome, you will realise that you have not done too badly after all.

In some ways, moving to a new district can ease some of the potential problems in this sphere. A whole new range of acquaint-ances – some of whom will become friends – will be available to you. In this situation you will be able to make a fresh start, and once again become part of a group, but this time without the constraints of employment. Again, this is very dependent on your personality. Some people will move to a new district and never speak to their neighbours other than the routine 'good morning'. Others will throw themselves into all the local activities that are available.

Whatever your circumstances, think and act positively. Many of your peers will be feeling similar changes in their lifestyle. It is good to get together occasionally to talk over old times as well as to discuss successes and failures in the adjustment to retirement. (You will notice how much better the 'positive thinkers' fare.)

RELATIONSHIP WITH CHILDREN

Earlier retirement these days may mean that teenage children are still either living entirely at home or arrive home at frequent intervals – perhaps with the conventional piles of dirty washing. This is an entirely different situation from that of 20 to 30 years ago when very few men retired until the age of 65, by which time their children were usually married with children of their own. There are three facets of life that have altered, giving rise to this increasingly common situation:

1. As we have seen, earlier retirement, for men especially, means that they are at home for good often in their late fifties, almost ten years earlier than their forefathers. As well as relationship considerations, financial aspects of young people's careers may have an impact here.

2. Many more young people today are continuing with further education, and so are more likely to be at home into their early twenties. Boys particularly – even if they are at work – seem to prefer living at home: no doubt home comforts and good cooking exert a pull here. Girls usually have more of a 'nesting' instinct (even in these feminist days) and cannot wait to get into a flat of their own.

3. The age of child-bearing has in general become later in successive generations: many people retiring today started their families almost a decade later than did their grandparents and therefore still have children around the house.

There are probably few households which have not had some problem or other with teenage children, be it merely arguments about staying out late or playing noisy music or the more serious and worrying problems of alcohol or drug abuse. This is no new problem. Growing up has always had its difficulties, even in the time of Socrates. But today's teenagers have to cope with many and diverse temptations, and this, in combination with an increase in permissiveness and a decrease in discipline, can cause – sometimes explosive – confrontations. Something you could well do without as you yourself face a changing lifestyle.

Each individual situation will obviously have to be coped with on its own merits, and there is no universal panacea for such problems. But for your own sanity's sake, if you are much embroiled with teenage problems, remember that children do grow up eventually. Stick to your principles of acceptable behaviour, and you will probably be pleasantly surprised in a few years' time how much you will be enjoying – yes, actually enjoying – your children's company.

Your situation may be different. Perhaps your children are married and away from home, perhaps with children of their own. This can be a time of much joy, with grandchildren eagerly coming to visit, and how glad you will be at these times that you are retired and can enjoy their company to the full. Being a grandparent is lots of fun – perhaps better than being a parent. When the going gets rough, or when you feel quite exhausted, you can always say that it is time they went home. Some people, however, and particularly women it seems, may have difficulty in coming to terms with the idea of being a grandparent. It seems that the very label, 'grandmother', means that life is nearly done. Probably they subconsciously still think of grandmothers as white-haired, wrinkled, immobile ladies who sit at home all day bemoaning the antics of the young. This is far from the truth in reality – today's grandmothers are full of life and activity, so much so that they are often taken for their daughters' elder sisters – occasionally to the daughter's disgust.

A word of warning on the grandparenting role. Do be sure that you do have a life of your own, and are not asked to care for your grandchildren all the time. Obviously there are circumstances in which you will want to help – times of illness, or a necessary job that takes both parents out of the house, for example – but beware the too frequent requests to baby-sit. Remember, you too have a life to live and hobbies and recreations of your own that you wish to pursue in the evenings. This can be particularly difficult if you decide, on retirement, to move to live nearer to your children – a factor to think about when you are considering moving, or not moving, house.

Financial help to your children can also affect the relationship you have with them. If you are in a fortunate enough position to be able to help financially, beware you do not undermine your children's confidence in their own abilities. It is hard indeed to see your children struggling along with a heavy mortgage when you could perhaps easily help them out. But you went through the same struggles at their age, and what a feeling of fulfilment it was to be able to manage on your own. Your children, too, must be allowed to feel this self-respect. One way in which grandparents can perhaps be helpful is by assisting with school fees, if this is an educational option that your children wish to pursue for their children. There are two main ways in which this can be done:

1. Making a Deed of Covenant. This will mean that regular payments are made to the parents on behalf of the child (in this case designated for the payment of school fees) and is advantageous to you if you are a taxpayer. Tax can be reclaimed on the amount convenanted yearly. Deeds of covenant usually last for seven years. Forms for convenanting purposes can be obtained from the Inland Revenue.

2. Giving a lump sum for this specific purpose. The most usual and convenient way is to pay a lump sum into an educational trust which guarantees to pay a certain level of school fees over a definite period. Further advice should be obtained from a financial advisor or from the Independent Schools Information Service (ISIS), 56 Buckingham Gate, London SW1E 6AG.

Our relationship with our children changes regularly over the years. What we all aim for is mutual dependence and loving friendship with another adult based on long years of love and respect as we ourselves get older. The prospect of retirement gives the opportunity to think carefully about how far we have progressed along this ideal road with our children.

RELATIONSHIP WITH ELDERLY PARENTS

This is perhaps one of the hardest relationships to get right as you yourself approach retirement. Earlier retirement exerts its influence in this sphere, as does the undoubted fact that we are all living longer. It is now more usual than unusual for retiring folk to have at least one parent still alive.

The presence in the family of an ageing relative will have effects on housing. Perhaps you will move to accommodate a parent in a 'granny flat'? Or maybe move to a different part of the country to be near enough to look after a parent who is becoming increasingly disabled? While we all have responsibilities in this direction, you also have needs. Will the new situation be as suitable for you as you get older? It is an unhappy solution to uproot yourself from a place in which you are happy, only to find, in a few years' time, that your elderly parent has to be moved to some form of sheltered accommodation.

Problems there certainly can be in these relationships but, alternatively, much pleasure can come out of a move to be near an elderly relative. If there are still teenage children in the family home, often these two generations – either side of you – can have much to offer each other. There can be an affinity between grandparent and grandchild which is quite impossible to achieve between parent and child. Who knows, this may be a way of counteracting – or at least diluting – teenage problems?

Decisions over the care of elderly parents who are finding it difficult to manage can be extremely worrying and disturbing. While you do not want to neglect your responsibilities, life can become an intolerable burden if the old person is particularly cantankerous. Do not hesitate to ask for help in these circumstances from your own doctor, who may ask a geriatrician (specialist in the care of the elderly) to help. The social services department can also help with such things as 'meals on wheels', aids to daily living in the home and perhaps attendance at a day centre.

Eventually you may think it wisest that your elderly parent is cared for either in wardened accommodation or in a residential home. Open discussion between everyone concerned about this possibility is a 'must' if relationships are not to deteriorate. It may just be that your elderly parent would prefer to move into an environment which is specifically geared to his or her needs, offering a slower pace and companions of the same age, but for reasons of loyalty, or not wishing to appear ungrateful, has not mentioned this possibility. Obviously you will search around for suitable, caring accommodation, not too far away so that you will be able to visit frequently.

Whatever you do, never feel guilty about the decision once it is made. You have thought carefully about it, and acted upon your decision – so it is the right one.

There are a number of organisations which can give you general help and advice on such matters:

Age Concern, 60 Pitcairn Road, Mitcham, Surrey CR4 3LL, telephone 01-640 5431.

Help the Aged, 16–18 St James's Walk, London EC1R 0BE, telephone 01-253 0253.

National Council for Carers and their Elderly Dependants, 29 Chilworth Mews, London W2 3RG, telephone 01-262 1451.

RELATIONSHIP WITH HUSBAND OR WIFE

This is the most important relationship of all as you approach retirement. As discussed in Chapter 1, the situations in which husband and wife can find themselves are many and varied. Wives working, husbands retired; husbands working, wives retired; both retired; a new marriage – the permutations are endless.

At this time of your life, your relationship will take on an entirely new phase. Give and take will be necessary on both sides before you finally settle down into a new pattern. Do not get too impatient with one another – you will both have to adapt to some extent. Above all, talk about the problems that you may both be finding. Keep a sense of humour – laugh at the odd things that happen to you. Try not to be too rigid in what you do, or expect your partner to do. The early days of retirement can seem like one long holiday, but once this 'honeymoon' period is over it is as well to bring some form of routine into your lives – times you spend together, times when you each pursue your own particular interest or hobby.

Many couples find that the intimate side of their marriage takes on a new fulfilment at this time. They have the time to make love gently and quietly without the demands of work or children. Worries about possible pregnancy have probably long since disappeared. The companionship of the years has led to a greater knowledge of each other's needs.

Sexual activity at this time often increases, and is one more good reason for keeping your body in as good a working order as possible. Positions for intercourse may have to be adjusted to accommodate a stiff back or a painful knee, for example, but with long years of companionship behind them, a happy, long-married couple will adapt to this with good humour. Two recent pieces of research have shown that sexuality in older couples does not decline, as was thought for so long. The very thought of anyone approaching sixty having sex was thought to be unlikely, wrong, or somehow distasteful: just how wrong this is has been justified by these reports. A passionate young couple will probably be a passionate middle-aged couple – and this will continue into old age. Even if full intercourse does not occur, older men and women need to be caressed and cuddled just as much as they did when they were younger. (Recently it was reported that a man who was sent off to work by his wife with a kiss could expect to live five years longer than the man who did not receive this sign of affection. This can doubtless be extended into the retirement age-group. Loving physical contact is good for us – at all ages.)

Divorce and remarriage can often be a fact of life for middle-agers today. Many people who have been through the trauma of divorce will find themselves thinking carefully about committing their lives to a further partnership. Remarrying in middle age can mean that in the very near future you will be spending a good deal more time together as retirement approaches. So be sure that you really do think alike on major issues. Thoughts may also occur about the possibility of the new partner becoming chronically ill or disabled. You must carefully weigh up these possible disadvantages – only 'possible', remember – against the companionship and intimate pleasures you will be able to share with your husband or wife. There are a number of facets that must be considered before making a final decision, and many will include personal and religious reasons. But many second marriages are satisfying and extremely happy.

Relationships depend to a large extend on basic personality and how one has viewed the world and coped with life through many years. Some people who have a tendency to anxiety and depression earlier in their lives find retirement, or even the prospect of it, difficult. They are the people who have always found adaptation to change worrying. Perhaps such changes have been accompanied by depressive feelings. It is important to distinguish between these temporary reactive depressive feelings (which affect us all at times) and a true depressive illness.

Reactive depression. There is often an easily seen reason for this – a change of lifestyle – loss of a loved one – change of living accommodation: in a susceptible person the causes are legion. Women are more often affected than men. Symptoms of this type of depression include:

1. A degree of associated anxiety with all its attendant symptoms – irritability, loss of appetite, maybe palpitations and diarrhoea.

2. An inability to concentrate on any one thing for long.

3. Feelings of misery and a lack of desire to do anything constructive.

4. Nightmares disturbing sleep.

These symptoms will frequently take the sufferer to the doctor and tranquillisers have all too frequently been prescribed to control the symptoms without any attempt to unravel the underlying cause. These drugs have their uses in the short term but repeated prescriptions can – and do – lead to a form of addiction. Fortunately this is now being recognised and more care is taken in the prescribing of these drugs.

With the sympathy of family and friends, and a certain degree of insight into the problem, these periods of reactive depression can be controlled. Also, as the sufferer gets older, she will be better able to recognise the onset of her depressive feelings, and so be able to ask for help early on in the condition. Everyone has events occurring in their lives which, understandably, give rise to reactive depression. Acknowledging this is half-way to coming to terms with your feelings.

Depressive illness. Here the symptoms are different from those associated with reactive depression.

1. The whole body mechanism is slowed during a depressive illness. Movement, thought and bodily functions all slow down and the sufferer will often sit for hours doing absolutely nothing – alone with his or her thoughts of misery.

2. Feelings of guilt, shame and unworthiness are uppermost, and suicide is often thought of, or attempted.

3. Sleep is disturbed. Getting to sleep at night is not as much of a problem as the early awakening. In the early morning hours, at the best of times, life can appear gloomy: the distress the sufferer from depression feels at these times can be devastating. Lack of adequate refreshing sleep leads to tiredness and lassitude the following day, thus compounding the problem.

4. Anxiety is nearly always an associated feature of depression. Sufferers are fearful of undertaking even the simplest actions – an easy train journey, for example, will throw them into a panic. They become tearful at the slightest provocation.

5. Changes of mood can also occur, and the person who has

been sitting in the same chair for days will suddenly start roaming the room, talking incessantly – usually about themselves and how they are feeling. After a while they will subside again into their previous almost somnolent state.

Treatment is along three main lines:

1. Drugs, which affect the physical aspects of the disease. There are a number of different types of these, all acting in a slightly different way. Some have unwanted side-effects, such as a rise in blood pressure, and this must be carefully monitored.

2. Electro-convulsive therapy, which is usually given in conjunction with the anti-depressive drugs. A course is usually five or six treatments, and many people benefit.

3. Psychotherapy, which involves delving into the feelings and apprehensions of the depressed person with the help of a skilled counsellor. As an awareness of the deeper feelings is achieved, the sufferer is able to make decisions about his or her own future. Dependence on the counsellor must be avoided and much skill is necessary to avoid this.

Friends and relatives can help the sufferer by aiding him or her to join in social activities once again. Inviting a depressed friend or relative to join you in some outing or activity can be of much help. If you meet with a refusal, do not be rebuffed – try again the next time something suitable turns up.

Having looked at the negative side of adapting to a new lifestyle, let us consider the positive aspects.

Mental agility is something that we all need to maintain as we get older. The old story that, as we lose so many million brain cells every year after twenty-five, by the time we retire our brains are useless has long since died an unmourned death. Our brains have much spare capacity – the only activity that is essential is to give them plenty to do. In retirement there can be a positive pleasure in engaging in activities we enjoy, rather than spending most of our waking hours in a job which has perhaps become routine and tedious.

How do *you* propose to keep your brain in the best possible trim? Perhaps a second career is ahead of you – opening a shop, running a guest-house, becoming the landlord of a pub or making a few pounds to add to your pension by using some skill you possess.

If a second career does not appeal to you (and remember it can be very hard work, and this may not be what you want at this time of your life) how about using your skills to help others?

Are you competent at:

- *Teaching*. Options open to you are
  helping in adult literacy programmes;
  helping handicapped people (blind, deaf) with study;
  part-time teaching at colleges of further education in your special interest subject;
  teaching at youth clubs; sportsmen and women are particularly welcome here.
- *Craft activities*
  make clothes, or knit garments, either for a local charity or someone who needs them;
  help in retirement homes with craft activities;
  help in hospitals with occupational therapy pursuits;
  teach your own particular craft to children or the elderly;
  learn more in depth about your own craft, maybe take up something entirely new if you are good with your hands generally.
- *Communication* (of all kinds)
  visit the old, the lonely or the depressed;
  maybe join the Samaritans;
  offer to write letters for disabled people;
  read books on to tape for the blind;
  write short stories for publication;
  assist at the local Citizens Advice Bureau;
  set up local neighbourhood watch schemes.
- *Artistic pursuits*
  learn more about your skill;
  exhibit your work locally;

offer to produce posters for local events;

help with musical activities at youth clubs/schools etc. if you are a musician;

join a choir if you enjoy singing.

- *Sport*

coach local youth clubs;

become involved in administration of local clubs as well as participating;

help arrange local fixtures or visits to national events.

- *DIY subjects*

help older people with the jobs they find difficult;

help younger people with problems around the house that they are too busy to attend to;

mend toys, play equipment at schools, hospitals, etc.

You can surely extend this list further. There is much that needs to be done by way of all kinds of voluntary work in this country today. Do not discount the possibility of performing some kind of voluntary work overseas – especially if you have retired early and are still in your fifties. VSO (Voluntary Service Overseas) is aware of the vast, untapped potential here, and is willing to send retired people off on two-year contracts to various parts of the world. The only proviso is that you are under sixty-five – and in good health.

Perhaps extending your skills in some direction appeals more to you. There is nothing like learning – or re-learning – a skill to keep your mind alert and in good trim. Why not extend those musical skills? Perhaps you gave up piano lessons when you were in your teens? Find a sympathetic teacher and start again. You will find that much of what you learned years ago will come back again very quickly, although practice will be needed to extend and stretch those stiffened fingers.

- Maureen did this when she took early retirement from her teaching post at 56. She had played the piano during her working years on odd occasions for school concerts and assemblies, but had always felt that her standard was low.

A friend who had suffered a back injury while nursing had recently started on a second career by taking a music teaching diploma. Maureen asked her if she would take her on as an older pupil. They had many happy hours together over the succeeding three years or so. Having so recently passed her own music teaching examinations, Ruth was a sympathetic teacher for Maureen, and her skills grew weekly. She took several Associated Board music examinations, and passed these with distinction. Finally, having passed Grade 8, Maureen hesitantly asked Ruth, 'Shall I follow your example and do the teaching diploma?'

So, on her sixtieth birthday, Maureen took her diploma examination – and again passed with flying colours. She now has a full list of pupils who enjoy coming to her to learn. She has successfully managed to combine her teaching and musical skills into a whole new career.

Perhaps the visual arts are more to your liking? Why not attend watercolour classes, or go on a painting holiday which combines tuition with a certain amount of practical experience? You will meet many other like-minded people on these holidays.

There are, of course, many other branches of artistic activity – handbell ringing, choral singing, pottery, weaving – the list is endless. You will be limited by what is available locally, but if you make enquiries you will surely find something that is of interest to you.

Joining societies of one kind or another is a further way of keeping mentally agile. History societies are to be found in most communities and are usually well supported. If you are near London, many more societies will be available to you. Many arrange lectures, visits and previews, and the subscription rate is reduced if you are in the older age bracket. Clubs exist, too, for such diverse hobbies as ornithology, photography, flower arranging and so on. Bridge and chess clubs abound in most parts of the country, and for outdoor pursuits, golf, bowls, badminton and gardening groups are available. There is rarely any need to stagnate mentally if you are willing to find out about local activities and then take the plunge and join in with something which interests you.

If you feel like studying some subject in real depth, the Open University is always available with a multitude of choices. About one in ten of Open University students are over 60. If you are interested write to the Open University, PO Box 71, Walton Hall, Milton Keynes MK7 6AG. Looking at the Open University timetables in the *Radio Times* will give you an idea of when programmes are on and the range of subjects available. Other courses can, of course, be done at your local college of further education, either during the day or in the evenings.

You can see that there are endless possibilities – many, many more than can be mentioned here – that can keep you mentally alert and also give you the assurance that you are still needed and have a valuable contribution to make to society. All those years of experience can be put to good use now that you have time – that most precious of commodities.

7 · Bereavement

Ostrich-like indeed would be the retirement age man or woman who, however briefly and dismissively, has not considered the loss of his or her partner. The oft-repeated cliché 'death is the one certain fact of life' is obviously true. We have all met death at some time in our lives – grandparents, parents, friends or, in some tragic cases, children. These losses are hard to bear, but the ultimate in bereavement is when a husband or wife dies. If the partnership has been a long, happy and loving one, the trauma can be devastating.

Various cultures view death very differently, according to religious belief – or lack of it. In the developed countries of the world, as expectations of health have risen and religious experience declined, the thought of death has been pushed aside. To discuss death in any personal way is taboo. So when the inevitable event does occur, many people have no experience or inner strength to help them through the grieving process.

This process is a very necessary one, if the bereaved person is to be able satisfactorily to come to terms with life again. Perhaps one of the most important facts to remember is that life *will* be worth living again, but in a different way. Trying to continue in the old familiar ways that were so comfortable and easy will not be helpful. Rather, the widow or widower must look at life in an entirely different light now that his or her status in the world has altered.

But before this can be attempted, the normal stages of grieving – and they are very specific for everyone – must be gone through. Grief must not be denied. Everyone will be affected differently, according to personality, belief and circumstances, but, nevertheless, there are six distinct stages of grief. These stages may be passed through quickly, or the bereaved person may return to one particular stage again and again. It is when one stage lasts for many weeks that difficulties with adjustment to the new state can arise.

1. Anticipation of the loved one's death. Obviously, in the case of sudden death through accident, heart attack or stroke in a previously seemingly healthy person, this stage will not occur. But in any illness, however short, the realisation usually comes to husband or wife that death may be the outcome.

At first sight this may seem to make the loss easier, but however expected the death may be, the shock when it does take place is still traumatic. If death comes to relieve much suffering, there is often a sense of relief which in turn can lead to feelings of guilt – see stage 3.

2. Complete numbness and lack of feeling commonly occur in the period immediately following the death. Often people will tell you later that they can remember very little of the time immediately following the death of a spouse.

● Madge lost her husband at an early age from a virulent cancer, when her two sons were still in their teens. She was an accomplished church organist. One day, years later, after playing at a funeral in the local church, she was asked what hymns she had chosen for her own husband's funeral. She had to admit that she had hardly any remembrance of the occasion and none whatsoever of the hymns that had been sung. One would have thought that with her musical ability, this fact at least would have stayed in her mind. But the numbness after the event had wiped her memory clean.

Actual physiological changes occur in the body following the death of a loved one. Appetite is lost, sleep comes only with difficulty and many of the body's normal functions are reduced to a very low ebb.

3. If death is unexpected or sudden, feelings of anger can be frighteningly severe. The bereaved person will blame any one of a number of factors – or people – involved around the time of the death.

Guilt feelings can also occur: 'Did I do enough during the last few weeks?' 'Perhaps if I had done more she would still be alive now?' This can occur particularly following a long, trying illness in which tiredness and worry have played havoc with the caring person's health.

The knowledge that you are not alone in harbouring these feelings can do much to help. A knowledgeable and sympathetic ear will do much to help the sufferer through this stage.

4. The stage of disbelief and denial can occur alongside or before the anger/guilt stage. The bereaved person knows objectively that the beloved is dead, but emotionally this cannot as yet be come to terms with. Momentarily, every person with a similar build or physique is thought to be the lost one.

These feelings can occur, at intervals, over many weeks until eventually:

5. Acceptance of the final fact of death occurs. Once this stage is reached the bereaved person is well on the road to recovery. He or she has 'let the loved one go', and no longer holds on to every tiny memory day by day. Other activities, without the loved one's presence, begin again to be undertaken. At this time:

6. Regrowth is well under way. Many months will pass before this is complete, and a new life is built up again. That is not to say that life will be the same as before – it never can be, and one should not want it to be. But interests and activities are taken up again, and the bereaved person slides back into society in his or her new role of widow or widower.

These stages of grief obviously do not occur in the simplified fashion described. They overlap and run into one another, and may be repeated time and time again before recovery finally occurs. Much help can be given throughout this time by sympathetic and knowledgeable friends. If you have a friend or a neighbour who has recently been bereaved, you can be a help to him or her, throughout their grieving.

Everyone can benefit from sympathy during their time of grief. Unfortunately in western society bereaved people tend to be shied away from, even to the extent of crossing the road so as to avoid speaking to a recently bereaved person: a sad fact of our youth-orientated society. It may be difficult to know just what to say, but a sympathetic 'I'm sorry' will do much to relieve the feeling of devastating loneliness the bereaved person is undoubtedly feeling. Ignoring him or her – or worst of all telling him 'to brace up and forget all about it' – will only increase the sense of isolation. There was a good deal of merit in the old-fashioned idea of a definite period of mourning in which the bereaved were treated gently and with sympathy. They were given all possible help at this time, but at the end of the mourning time would be expected to take charge of their lives again, and 99 times out of 100 it worked.

As with other 'life events' – birth and marriage – there are a number of things that must be done. Dealing with these statutory obligations, together with other positive actions, can be of assistance in the grieving process.

1. A death certificate must be obtained from the doctor who was caring for the person at the time of death – your own doctor if the death occurred at home or the hospital doctor if the death occurred there. If the death was sudden or unexpected, or was surrounded by any unusual circumstances, the doctor must report this to the coroner for the district before issuing a death certificate. The coroner may ask for a post-mortem examination to be performed, and his decision is final on this matter. The post-mortem will definitively decide the cause of death. Depending on the circumstances and the result of the post-mortem, an inquest may or may not be held. Post-mortems and inquests are rarely called for, and after most deaths the attending doctor will be able to issue a death certificate.

If you opt for cremation, a second, independent doctor will have to examine the body and sign the necessary form. Your own doctor will guide you through this if you tell him of your wish for cremation.

2. The death will have to be registered, usually by the nearest relative, at the local office for the registration of births and deaths. Your doctor will be able to tell you where this is if you do not know.

This should be done as soon as possible after the receipt of the death certificate.

3. Funeral arrangements – burial or cremation – will have to be made. This will depend very much on the wishes of the family and the local facilities. Do not be surprised at the expense of a funeral these days: at least £400 to £500 will be necessary for the simplest arrangements. A death grant is available for everyone to help with funeral expenses. This is £30 at the present time. Many people provide some sort of refreshment after the service. Funerals are often times when families meet up again after many years, especially in these days when they no longer live for generation after generation in the same town or village. Promises are so often made at such gatherings to meet more frequently under happier circumstances, but it is very often another funeral (or maybe a wedding – a much more cheerful occasion) that brings the family together again.

4. Financial considerations will need to be sorted out after the three statutory procedures have been concluded. Insurances taken out against death must be searched out and realised. There is no immediate hurry to do this, on the day of the funeral for example, but it will have to be sorted out in the near future, and solicitors and accountants may need to be contacted on these aspects.

Bereavement, as we have seen, is usually accompanied by changes in body function of one sort or another. Difficulties with sleeping and eating are very common at this time. While it is not suggested that drugs should be used to muffle the degree of grief, or to diminish the important grieving process, some sleep is also of importance. A week's supply of sleeping pills to be taken at night can be useful in helping the sleeping pattern back to normal. Most general practitioners will give the necessary prescription if you explain your sleeping problems. A few hours away from the consciousness of your grief will prepare you better for the problems of the next day than another sleepless night. Appetite will return to normal within a few weeks. Meanwhile be sure you drink plenty of fluids – tea, in Britain at least, is the conventional panacea, but milky drinks can also be valuable at night, to help sleep and to provide some form of nourishment.

Once the first few sad weeks are over and the initial stages of grief are passing, regrowth must be actively considered. Now is the time to plan different activities – going away for a weekend break, attending an evening class on a subject that interests you, visiting friends and so on. All these first steps, without a loved partner, will not be easy, but once the initial hurt is over, interest in life *can* begin again – never the same as before, but still with enjoyment.

The first year following a bereavement is always the most difficult. Once each anniversary – be it birthday, Christmas or an annual holiday – is passed, other experiences will be available to recall other than memories of your loss.

What about actions that are definitely counterproductive or unwise to undertake during the grieving time?

1. Some people find it difficult to consider still living in the same house, while others cherish their shared home and find great comfort in familiar places and objects. Whichever way you are affected, it is unwise to make any major decisions, such as selling a house or giving up comfortable rented accommodation, until at least six months have passed since your bereavement. Your vision is not too clear at this time, and you have to work through the stages of your grief. Once sold, a house cannot be bought back again, however much you may wish to do so.

Similarly, invitations to live with your children or other relatives should be resisted at this time. This is a major step to undertake, and one which you may regret after a year or so, once you have begun to pick up the threads of life again. A short stay with relatives is a different matter, but any more permanent arrangements should definitely be postponed for a while.

2. Do not try to deny your grief, either to yourself or the outside world. Suppressed grief can result in a depressive-like illness at a later date. This is not to say that the bereaved person should

dissolve into tears at the slightest expression of sympathy, but admission of feelings of loneliness and missing the absent partner will aid the working through of the grief, and stimulate sympathetic understanding in others.

3. Hanging on to the old lifestyle is also counterproductive. Many of the old ways and habits need two to be complete, and endeavouring to continue with these will only add to the sense of loss. Once the acute grief symptoms have subsided, try to develop new habits and interests. This will do much to hasten the recovery process.

4. Finally, do not become a recluse. It can be very easy to stay around the house all day in bedroom slippers if you do not *have* to go out, but definitely not good for a satisfactory life in the years that remain to you. Accept those invitations that come your way – remember that after two or three refusals they probably will not come again. For people looking on at the bereaved person's struggles – do include your bereaved friend or relative in your activities. It may not be easy to invite a 'singleton' (that awful word that so aptly describes someone on their own), but with a little tact and sympathy – and perhaps finding someone else in a similar situation to invite – you will be helping your friend over a very difficult hurdle in his or her battle for regrowth.

As we get older, the fact of death becomes more of a reality, and perhaps it is easier to come to terms with than at a younger age. But on the opposite side, the older one is when separation occurs, the more difficult adaptation to a new lifestyle becomes. Widows tend to fare better than widowers after bereavement: two reasons spring to mind. Firstly, it is more usual for the male partner to die first. (Average life expectancy for men is about seven years less than it is for women.) So there are many more 'fellow widows' around with whom to mix. Secondly, women tend to be more content with activities around the house and garden than do men, particularly the present generation of older women. Maybe this will change in succeeding generations, as those women who are used to full-time careers come up to widowhood. Interesting to ponder how the feminist movement will cope with this aspect of life.

Finally, remember that grief is an active process through which a bereaved person must pass. There is a pattern – as with all other life events – which with sympathetic help and understanding can be worked through to a satisfactory conclusion.

8 · Benefits of retirement

Many differences face the about-to-be, or recently, retired person – in financial affairs, in housing, in health, in lifestyle. Having checked through all these, it is a good idea to sit down with a pencil and paper and list all the benefits of retirement, as they apply to you. Be honest – leave out those aspects which you personally do not think are beneficial (but which may in fact turn out to be so). In spite of this, you will probably be surprised at the factors which are beneficial to you. You will probably be able to think of many more, but here are a few thoughts on the subject, together with a few tips on how to make the most of these benefits.

TIME

This is the one thing that – theoretically at least – we should have more of in retirement, yet how often does one hear people, who have planned their retirement in a positive way, say that they seem to have less time now than when they were working? But how different is the way in which they spend their time. Instead of having to go out every day to earn a livelihood, the time is spent on doing things that interest you, and which you really enjoy doing. (If you are no longer enjoying doing what you spend your time on in retirement, remember that you are quite at liberty to give it up.)

Do you realise that if you have worked an average eight-hour day, five days a week for forty-eight weeks of the year, on retirement you will have almost 2000 extra hours every year to spend in doing what you please? Daunting? Or exciting? By planning and thinking positively the latter option can definitely be yours. A few ways in which you could spend your extra time are:

1. Spending more time with your family. And not just your

husband, wife or children. Why not arrange a get-together for all the branches of your extended family? This could be the time when you really do fulfil all those promises that are so often made at weddings and funerals.

● Helena and Kenneth did this following the funeral of Kenneth's father in February. 'Instead of just talking about it,' Helena had stated firmly, 'we will all get together just for the sake of catching up on family news – the day will be the 29th July at our house!'

Kenneth had been very sceptical at the idea – especially as it involved over 30 people. But as 29 July drew nearer, he realised that his wife had been as good as her word, beavering away, on the telephone and by letter, making all the arrangements. Difficulties with 90-year-old Aunt Edith's immobility had seemed insurmountable at first, but a second cousin, visiting from Australia, heard of the family gathering and offered to transport Aunt Edith in the Dormobile hired for the stay.

It was Helena who was having second thoughts as July drew towards its close: Kenneth was looking forward to reminiscing with aunts, uncles and cousins. Food and talk were available in abundance on the day. The weather was fine, many happy memories were shared, and new friendships were made between distant cousins who previously had only heard of each other's existence.

The person who probably enjoyed it most of all was Aunt Edith. She spent most of her day laughing with members of her large family, and was heard to remark as she was wheeled back into the Dormobile: 'One of the best days of my life!'

Perhaps this large-scale entertaining is not something you would care to embark upon too frequently, but why not spend a day visiting those cousins you have not seen for years, now that you are retired? Maybe, too, retirement is a time for healing old family rifts that have occurred, and dragged on, over the years.

2. In the same way, retirement is a good time to look up old friends. The pressures of working life are often such that there is

very little time in which to journey to another part of the country –
maybe even to a different country. Friends of your own age are
probably also on the brink of retirement. It is good to compare
notes, and perhaps to pick up again the similar interests that
attracted you to each other years ago.

3. New acquaintances, too, may develop further into friendship as you have time to spend together pursuing a common
interest. Why not have a regular supper/coffee morning/barbecue
for local neighbours who have reached a similar time of life to
yourself? Perhaps you could link this with some fund-raising
activity for a charity in which you are interested? Many new ideas
can come out of such meetings. It could be that someone of
retirement age in the next street would like to set up a small
business, for example, but needs a partner with whom to share?

4. What about starting off on a completely new track – a
business of your own: a bed-and-breakfast establishment, a pub, a
corner shop or 'going commercial' on some aspect of handicraft?

Great care must be taken if you are seriously considering this
option. Many are the pitfalls – financial, premises, staffing problems etc. – and remember the aim is to have a new interest, not to
go from one state of overwork to another. Ask yourself a few
pertinent questions before you set out on this path:

Is there scope in your town/village for this type of project?

Have you the special skills/knowledge necessary?

Can you raise sufficient initial capital?

Can you ensure that your standard of living will not drop?

Will it use up all of your precious free time?

How will it affect the rest of your family?

Are you fit enough to cope with the added work the venture
will undoubtedly produce?

If you can satisfactorily allay any fears on these (and maybe
other) points, go ahead. Many, many people are thoroughly
enjoying their second careers.

5. If you feel that paid work/running a business is not for you,
why not consider some form of voluntary work? There are organ-

isations by the score that will be only too glad of your services. What you decide on will, of course, be determined by the situation where you live and also by your own special skills and experience. It is important that you use skills and knowledge that you have built up over the years, however much you think you would like to do something entirely different, and do not forget that the sum total of your skills does not comprise only those you used in your paid work. What about other interests – music, gardening, carpentry, crafts of all kinds? Many of these skills can be used to help other people.

REACH (Retired Executive Clearing-House), 89 Southwark Street, London SE1 0HD, telephone 01-928 0452, is an agency which matches skills gained in commerce to similar needs in a wide range of charities. Your expenses will be reimbursed by most charitable concerns, but no salary is given.

St John Ambulance, or Red Cross, always need people who are interested in learning about first aid. Enquire at your Citizens Advice Bureau about local branches.

The National Council for Voluntary Organisations, headquarters at 26 Bedford Square, London WC1B 3HU, telephone 01-636 4066, is an organisation which can put you in touch with charities and organisations that are in need of help. If there is no local branch near you, a call to headquarters will set you off on the right track.

6. Pets may seem a trivial consideration. But have you longed for a dog all your working life, and not been able to own one owing to the demands of a heavy working schedule? If so, now is the time to think about acquiring one – but first of all be sure you are fully aware of all that keeping a pet entails.

Dogs need to be fed/groomed/exercised on a regular daily basis.

Dogs and cats need to be accommodated when you are away on holidays/weekend visits. Maybe you can take your pet with you/leave it with a friend or relative/leave it in suitable kennels?

It will cost an appreciable sum of money to keep a pet. As well as food, you must consider necessary inoculations and vet's fees should this be necessary at any time.

A fair commitment of time and organisation, but the benefits can be well worth your trouble:

Companionship, especially if you live alone.

Provides a focus for getting into a routine – again an especially important function if you are on your own.

Can often help to make new acquaintances – dogs, like babies, are excellent conversation openers!

A dog can be a good guard for both you and your property – not necessarily in a vicious way, but merely to warn that strangers are around, and to deter opportunist thieves.

There have been shown to be health advantages in owning a dog, as well as the benefit of having to exercise the animal. Blood-pressure and heart rate have been shown to be reduced by stroking a dog (or a cat, of course).

Research has shown that there may be a positive link with a long life. Pet owners tend to reach an older age in a healthier physical and mental state than other people, and recovery after illness has also been shown to be improved among pet owners.

There are, of course, many other pets that you can own as well as a dog or cat. Fish and birds are also sources of interest and commitment, and may be more suitable to your living conditions. (But for my money, dogs win hands down every time.) There are many beautiful, loving animals waiting to be rescued from animal homes all over the country. Contact your local branch of the RSPCA for where to find the home nearest to you, or any veterinary surgeon will be able to put you in touch.

You will certainly be able to think of any number of other ways in which to enjoy the extra 2000 hours a year that you now have available. You will then probably be joining the ranks of those retired people who say they never have enough time to fit everything in!

TRAVEL

Perhaps you have always longed to see the far-flung corners of the world. Or perhaps a more intimate knowledge of one corner of your homeland appeals to you more? Now is the time to indulge yourself, perhaps with a portion of your 'lump sum' for a long-range holiday, perhaps with several shorter breaks nearer to home out of income. Remember that if you are in the senior citizen bracket, there are a number of travel concessions open to you (see Chapter 3).

Many more people today see an annual holiday as a necessity, not as the luxury that it was a generation or so ago. Now that you are retired, or planning to retire, holidays will no longer be restricted to a two-week break between long weeks of work. A holiday can be taken for the sake of an interest or to pursue some hobby rather than for a well-earned rest.

1. One of the great advantages of retirement (and of being freed from any necessity to take your holiday in school holiday times) is that many firms offer bargain holidays, both at home and abroad during off-peak seasons. Add to these savings your own concessionary rates of travel and you may well be able to afford a number of holidays every year, and it is often more pleasant at these quieter times of the year. Remember, too, looking at the other side of the coin, that many universities (often in beautiful parts of Britain) offer cheap accommodation during the college vacation. An added bonus can be the use that can be made of the campus facilities, such as the swimming pool, badminton courts and so on. Specialised holidays are also available, for example painting, rambling, history courses, at these venues.

2. Investigate specialised holidays for the over-55s. Bulk buying of accommodation – and this can also include accommodation on cruise liners – can result in a sizeable reduction in the price of the holiday. Other advantages include:

The companionship of people of a similar age to yourself – especially helpful for men and women on their own.

Activities and talks that are geared to your age group.

No noisy music to disturb the peace of the small hours of the morning – an undoubted hazard in many holiday resorts.

Consideration will have been given to the availability of door-to-door transport, and ease of access to places of interest near to the hotel.

A number of companies cater for the older traveller, and the following are only a small selection:

Saga Holidays, Saga Buildings, Middelburg Square, Folkestone, Kent CT20 1AZ, telephone 0303 40000. Holidays are arranged for most parts of the world, including Japan, the USSR and Australia.

Thomson 'Young at Heart' Holidays, Greater London House, Hampstead Road, London NW1 7SD, telephone 01-387 9321.

The Promised Land Senior Citizens Tour, Willson's Hall, Willson's Road, Ramsgate, Kent CT11 9LZ, telephone 0843 583164. This firm specialises in group tours to Israel and is geared to the physical needs of more mature travellers.

In Britain, information on off-peak travel can be obtained from:

English Tourist Board, Thames Tower, Black's Road, London W6 9EL, telephone 01-846 9000.

Scottish Tourist Board, 23 Ravelston Terrace, Edinburgh EH4 3EO, telephone 031-332 2433.

Wales Tourist Board, Brunel House, 2 Fitzalan Road, Cardiff CF2 1UY, telephone 0222 499909.

Finally, Cruse, the national organisation for the widowed, also have a list of suitable holidays. Their address is 126 Sheen Road, Richmond, Surrey TW9 1UR, telephone 01-940 4818. You will also be able to obtain further information from your usual travel agent or from specialist magazines, such as *Fifty Plus* or *Choice*.

Having decided where you are going this year (maybe more than one holiday?), what are the things to remember about travel specifically now that you are in the older age bracket? (All the normal things, such as the safety of your home and valuables, care of pets and gardens etc., will be second nature to you after a lifetime of holidays.) Basically this comes down to your health when travelling. Long-term chronic illness – particularly those illnesses related to heart or lungs, or those which affect mobility – may make a few extra precautions necessary, particularly if you are travelling by air.

There are a few conditions – some temporary – which will make air travel unwise. So bear these in mind when you are planning your holiday.

1. *Heart conditions*

You should not fly on a commercial airline within three weeks of suffering a coronary thrombosis.

Similarly, flying should be avoided for 3 weeks after a stroke.

Any person with a *serious* vascular or blood pressure problem would be unwise to fly.

The reasons for these restrictions are that during high-altitude flying – above 22,000 feet – the partial pressure of oxygen cannot be maintained at atmospheric pressure. For people who have long-term vascular or lung conditions oxygen should always be available on the flight. If you think this may apply to you, consult your own doctor, who will inform the airline of your condition. (A form, MEDIF, is obtainable for this purpose from travel agents for British Airways flights.)

If you have any condition giving rise to a *severe* degree of anaemia, flying should be avoided until this has been corrected. Under these circumstances there will be insufficient haemoglobin in the red blood cells to carry adequate oxygen to the tissues.

2. *Abdominal conditions*

Flying should be avoided for three weeks after any abdominal surgery.

Following any bleeding from the digestive tract (from, for example, an ulcer or from a bout of diverticulitis), it is unwise to fly for at least three weeks after the last bout of bleeding.

People with colostomies should be prepared with an extra spare bag.

3. Upper respiratory tract conditions

The sufferer from a severe congestive head cold would be wise to postpone his flight for a day or two if at all possible until the worst stage is over. This is, of course, not always possible when a flight has been booked for many weeks. The use of a decongestant immediately before take-off can be helpful, but be prepared for some degree of pain in the sinuses and ears during the climb to altitude.

Similarly, any acute sinusitis or ear infection should be treated adequately before flying.

4. *Fractures* which are immobilised by a plaster should be treated with caution before flying. Owing to the pressure differences any air trapped under the plaster can expand, and cause pain. More seriously, the leg or arm can swell and so increase the pressure inside the plaster, reducing the blood supply to the limb. This can cause severe pain. In these circumstances it may be necessary to split the plaster, and then have it reapplied when you reach your destination.

5. *Serious infectious disease.* This is an obvious contraindication to flying. With the speed and ease of modern travel, infectious disease can be spread – literally – round the world within a few hours.

It is to be hoped that none of these conditions will be affecting you as you plan a holiday. Your doctor will be able to advise you should you have any doubts about flying. Most airlines have a medical department, and will also be able to give advice.

Immunisations against specific diseases are recommended for travel to some parts of the world. Your own general practitioner will have an up-to-date list of which immunisation procedures are currently advised for different areas: very few are compulsory, but it is obviously in your own interests to avoid infection as far as possible. Changes do occur from time to time and require-ments vary, so it is always wise to check. There are five conditions against which immunisation, or protection, should be considered.

1. *Tetanus*

One injection followed by another in one month and then a further injection in six months will be necessary if you have never been immunised against tetanus before. If you have received a full course at any time in the past (even when you were a child or in the forces) only one 'booster' injection will be necessary.

Before travelling to any part of the world you should check that your tetanus protection is up-to-date. (And especially so if you are a gardener, you should check about this protection anyway – travelling or not. A 'booster' dose is advisable every ten years.)

2. *Polio*

A full course, if you have not already received this, consists of three drops of vaccine on a lump of sugar every month for three months. If you have previously received a full course, only a 'booster' of three drops will be necessary. A 'booster' dose is advisable for many parts of the world. Only countries which have had a good immunisation policy are exempt. These include most of the European countries, Majorca, Minorca, the USA and the Canary Islands.

3. *Typhoid*

Two injections with one month in between – to be repeated every three years if you are a regular traveller. This immunisation is advisable for many parts of the world – again with the exception of the countries where polio immunisation is not necessary.

4. *Cholera*

Two injections with four to six weeks in between injections. This protection only lasts six months, and is of doubtful value. It is better to rely on good hygiene, that is, not to drink any water unless you are sure that it is safe to do so, and to be sure to peel any fruit you may eat. This immunisation is necessary, as a general rule, for those countries where typhoid and polio immunisations are also required.

5. *Hepatitis*

One injection four days before travel. This must not be given before polio or yellow fever immunisation, and not less than two weeks after these immunisations. So, if you are travelling to a part of the world where this protection is necessary, you must be sure to start on your immunisations in good time before your travel date. Gamma-globulin as a protection against hepatitis is advisable for travel in the remoter corners of the world, and in those countries that are currently involved in a war, or if you are travelling rough.

REDUCTION OF STRESS

This is perhaps one of the greatest benefits of retirement, difficult to measure in any quantitative form, but nevertheless very real. No longer need you worry about deadlines, reports to meetings, staffing problems and all the multitude of stressful situations that make up working life.

Some degree of stress is thought to be important in keeping mentally alert, but the grinding rat-race that many of today's workers suffer is quite beyond this minimal level. Because life without some form of challenge (which implies some degree of stress) is not conducive to mental agility, it is vital to have interests and activities when you retire, as we have seen, so do not avoid speaking at that local government meeting or taking that music or language examination simply because this will entail some stress. It will keep you on your mettle, but without undermining your health as does the continuing stress so many working people are submitted to today.

As a spin-off from this respite from excessive stress, you will probably find that your general health is much improved – even without a fitness campaign. The ability to take it easy when you feel especially over-tired, or perhaps suffering from a common cold, does much to improve health levels. It has been remarked many times that people in their sixties often enjoy robust health, and this must, in part, be due to the retired state. This will depend very much, though, on the attitude of mind that you bring to retirement, or the approach of it.

*   *   *

Think positively about this phase in your life; plan long-term and also on a daily basis; give a little thought to your own physical, mental and spiritual needs and you will be able to say honestly that, 'the best is yet to be.'

Appendix · Health checklist

This appendix is in no way meant to be a self-diagnostic section. Your doctor must be the one to whom you turn if you feel unwell or have any symptoms that concern you. Rather, explanations are intended to reinforce what your doctor has told you, and be a reference point to which you can turn to refresh your memory on some aspects of your condition.

The section is arranged alphabetically for ease of reference only, not in order of the importance or seriousness of the diseases. The selection of conditions is also not exhaustive: that would need several text-books of medicine.

ANAEMIA

There are many causes of anaemia, which basically means a reduction in the oxygen-carrying power of the blood. This is measured by the amount of haemoglobin present – haemoglobin being the oxygen-binding substance in the red blood cells.

Signs and symptoms. Feelings of tiredness, lassitude and irritability may be due to anaemia. These feelings, combined with pale mucous membranes – inside lower eyelids and inside the mouth – should cause you to check whether you may be anaemic. (A pale skin of itself does not necessarily indicate anaemia. This may just be the type of skin you were born with. But everyone's mucous membranes should be a healthy, pink colour.)

In the retirement age group there are two main causes of anaemia.

1. Iron deficiency anaemia. Iron is necessary for the proper binding power of haemoglobin. There are four ways in which iron can be available in insufficient quantities:

a) Due to an insufficient intake in food. Foods rich in iron are red meats, liver and green vegetables (no extra in spinach). Adequate helpings of these foods will ensure that an iron-deficiency anaemia due to this cause is avoided.

b) Due to tiny amounts of blood being lost continually from the bowel. A gastric or duodenal ulcer, which perhaps does not give you much trouble, but which nevertheless may be bleeding sufficiently on a regular basis to lower the haemoglobin count may be the cause. A hiatal hernia (see below) can also be a source of small amounts of blood being lost on a regular basis.

c) Due to inadequate absorption of iron from the bowel. Some people's digestive tracts become less efficient as they get older, and do not absorb certain substances from food in adequate amounts in spite of a reasonable intake.

d) Due to excessive loss of blood in the monthly period by some women at the menopause.

Treatment is by investigating, and then remedying, the cause of the anaemia. Iron in tablet or liquid form is given daily to build up the body's supply again. Occasionally it is necessary to give extra iron by injection if the level has fallen too low.

Taking iron by mouth is not without its problems. Some people find that it gives them diarrhoea, others may become constipated. These effects can be reduced to a minimum by taking the tablets with a meal. If you do get side-effects from taking iron, tell your doctor: there are a number of equally good iron compounds which can be tried. You may need to take iron for some time. And remember that if you have the old feelings of tiredness returning after a course of treatment, do get your doctor's advice, together with a blood test, again.

2. Pernicious anaemia is due to an insufficient intake of vitamin B_{12}. Again this can occur in middle age due to defective absorption of this particular vitamin, found in green vegetables, eggs and liver.

The symptoms are similar to those of an iron-deficiency anaemia. It is only by a blood test that the actual type of the anaemia present can be determined.

Treatment today is by a monthly injection of vitamin B_{12}, after the levels have been raised by more frequent dosage. (We are fortunate indeed that this injection has been made possible. The previous treatment was for the sufferer to eat a sizeable quantity of *raw* liver every day.)

Anaemia due to either of these common causes is an immensely treatable condition. Although it may need long-term treatment, such treatment will improve immeasurably the quality of life.

ARTHRITIS

Arthritis means different things to different people. Some will say that they have arthritis if they have a few twinges in one or two of their joints in the mornings, while others *know* that they have arthritis by the boring, unremitting pain they feel in many of their joints as they try to pursue as normal a life as possible. Undoubtedly they are both right, but this simply shows how widely the severity of the condition can vary.

There are two types of arthritis – the word means, literally, inflammation in the joints. The causes of these two conditions are different; they affect different groups of people; affect different age-groups; have different courses of progression; and will need different forms of treatment.

OSTEO-ARTHRITIS

This is the condition in the joints, due to general 'wear and tear', which afflicts most of us to some degree by the time retirement age is reached. Even people in their late thirties and early forties can be found to have minimal signs of arthritis. Men and women are equally affected.

Signs and symptoms. Painful, creaking joints are the prime signs and symptoms of osteo-arthritis. Knees can become swollen and stiff. The joints usually found to be affected most severely are the big, weight-bearing joints such as the knees and the hips. Several factors have a bearing on the severity of the condition:

1. Any previous injury to a joint or a limb will tend to exacerbate osteo-arthritis in the affected joint. For example, a fracture of a leg requiring several weeks in plaster can set the scene for osteo-arthritis in nearby joints later in life.

2. Overweight, too, will carry its penalty in this direction. Hips and knees will bear the burden of those extra pounds with each step you take.

3. Poor posture will throw excess strain on particular parts of the joints. If your posture is good, weight will be distributed evenly over the whole surface of the joints.

The smaller joints of the wrists and fingers are not exempt from osteo-arthritis. In many older people you will notice small, knobbly swellings around the top joints of the fingers. (These are known as 'Heberden's nodes'.) They are due to a reaction in the bone surrounding the joint in response to the osteo-arthritis, almost as if your body is trying to protect the joint against excessive use by making it less mobile.

But it is when osteo-arthritis in the hips and knees becomes severe that effects on daily living are seen. Movements become slow and painful, and even getting up from a chair can be a major undertaking. Fortunately the disease is a relatively slow process, and not something that will afflict you overnight. So, think positively: avoid overweight, make sure your weight is distributed evenly over your joints by good posture and be sure that after any injury your muscles are exercised so that they are in full working trim again, and osteo-arthritis will have minimal effects on your life.

Treatment. Pain-killing and anti-inflammatory drugs are the mainstay of treatment in osteo-arthritis. Your doctor will plan a regime which is especially suited to your needs. There is often a period of trial and error with various drugs before a particular combination is found to suit you and keep you as pain-free and mobile as possible. There are a number of new anti-inflammatory drugs which can be very beneficial.

Physiotherapy is also very helpful both in maintaining the mobility of joints and building up strength in the muscles surrounding the affected areas. Keep-fit classes – as long as you do not overstrain your joints – are also of value.

If the damage to hip joints is very great, a hip replacement operation may be advised. Here the joint is completely replaced by an artificial metal hip-joint. Results of this operative procedure are excellent, although, unfortunately, in many places there are long waiting lists.

Osteo-arthritis need not be an insurmountable problem if you take steps to minimise its effects, starting as early as possible – and certainly by the time you are approaching retirement.

RHEUMATOID ARTHRITIS

This is quite a different disease from osteo-arthritis. The cause has yet to be unravelled. Viruses, stress and allergy have all been implicated, but, as yet, there is no one definitive answer. In contrast to osteo-arthritis, the smaller joints of the body – fingers, ankles and wrists – are more commonly involved and are acutely inflamed, although larger joints – hips and knees – can also suffer. The disease is more likely to attack women than men. The condition can start early in life and can also attack people in their seventies, but the most usual age of onset is around the forties and fifties.

Signs and symptoms

1. The onset can be sudden, or can come on gradually over weeks and months.

2. Pain can be severe and the range of movement of the affected joints can be very much diminished. Fingers are often the first joints to be affected, and a typical appearance of an affected finger is one with a swollen joint in the middle of the finger, giving rise to a spindle-shaped joint.

3. The affected joints are stiff, especially in the mornings after a

night's inactivity. This is in direct contrast to the picture seen in osteo-arthritis where the pain is worse after activity.

4. If the disease is severe, other systems of the body can be affected, and the unfortunate sufferer feels wretched and ill.

5. The general pattern of the disease is one of worsening followed by improvement. In many cases the disease can be quiescent for months or years.

Treatment. The aim is four-fold:

1. To reduce pain and inflammation during the acute stage of the disease. Pain-killers and anti-inflammatory drugs are the mainstay here. There are a number of relatively new drugs which have excellent results. The steroid drugs have to be used – for short periods of time only – in some severe cases. (Treatment with these drugs must be limited, owing to their side-effects.)

2. During the active, acute phase of the disease, it is important to keep joints in a good position so that deformity is kept to a minimum. Night-time splinting of wrists and knees with light-weight plastic splints is helpful in this direction.

3. Rest, with only gentle movements of the affected joints when they are acutely, and painfully, inflamed is an important part of treatment.

4. When the disease has become quiescent – and this may be after a few weeks or it may take several months – gentle exercises under the guidance of a physiotherapist should be taught. From this time on, it will be very much up to you to keep your joints as mobile as possible and to tone up your muscles to protect the affected joints.

Rheumatoid arthritis is an unpleasant disease, but one in which you can help yourself a good deal once the acute phase is over. Arthritis Care, 6 Grosvenor Crescent, London SW1X 7ER, gives valuable advice and help.

BRONCHITIS

Bronchitis is an inflammation of the bronchi – the cartilaginous tubes running down into the lung tissue. Bronchitis can arise as a complication of a cold – the cold going 'down on to the chest'. This can, of course, happen in any age group, but as we get older it is more likely to occur owing to a poorer breathing pattern, bad posture and/or damage done to lungs earlier in life. Work in a dusty atmosphere – coalminers are a prime example of this; severe lung infection when younger – a severe attack of whooping-cough in children can lead to permanent chest problems, including recurrent bronchitis when older; and, of course, smoking. Heavy cigarette smoking throughout life not only adds to the risk of lung cancer and heart attack, but also to chronic bronchitis. A morning 'smoker's cough' is just one sign of this. So, at the risk of being repetitive, do please give up smoking if you have not already done so. *Very* difficult to do, I know, but try one of the many 'help' methods that are around, from anti-smoking clinics through chewing-gums to hypnosis. Once you have broken the habit you really will feel better in many ways.

Signs and symptoms. Chronic bronchitis is characterised by:

1. a persistent cough;
2. the bringing up of phlegm;
3. breathlessness.

All these symptoms are due to the tiny air-passages being thickened and filled with secretions so that the air cannot get in and out easily. The breathlessness is particularly noticeable when extra demands are made on breathing when you have to run, for example, for a bus. Acute attacks of bronchitis can supervene. At these times the cough will worsen, breathlessness will increase, a fever may develop and the poor sufferer will feel wretched. Further damage to the lungs can be done over the years by chronic bronchitis. The walls of the alveoli (millions of tiny pouches in the lungs where the actual gaseous exchange takes place) become stretched and inelastic, so that air stagnates in them. This condition is known as 'emphysema', and can markedly restrict breathing.

Treatment. Things to do yourself include:

1. stop smoking;
2. lose weight if you are overweight;
3. take daily exercise – within your capabilities – to improve your lung capacity.

During an acute attack of bronchitis, you should contact your doctor, who will prescribe antibiotics to help control the infection. Some doctors advise permanent antibiotics for chronic bronchitis, others prefer to leave this form of treatment for an acute attack. Some advise immunisation against influenza in the autumn for all their patients who have a chronic chest problem.

The Chest, Heart and Stroke Association, Tavistock House North, Tavistock Square, London WC1L 9JE have excellent booklets on bronchitis and how best to cope with this condition.

CANCER

Cancer is not a disease entity in the same way as the other conditions that are being discussed. Rather, it is a generic name for a large number of diseases with a common factor – namely, that there is an uncontrolled growth of cells in a specific part of the body. So there is no one symptom on which you can put your finger and say that this is likely to be cancer. The picture is further complicated by the fact that cancers differ in the type of cells they contain. This in turn has an effect on how quickly or how slowly the cancer will grow.

A few facts and figures may put cancer – the disease that so many of us fear beyond all others – into its correct perspective.

1. Only between 15 and 20 per cent of deaths in the older age-group are due to cancer.
2. Cancers arising late in life tend to be slower growing than do those in the younger age-group.
3. Heredity plays a part. Families who do not have a history of

cancer are less likely to suffer from cancer in succeeding generations than those families many of whose ancestors had cancer.

4. If discovered and treated early, many forms of cancer are curable.

On the reverse side of the coin, however, there are two specific cancers that are more common in the retirement age group. These are breast cancer in women and prostatic cancer in men.

BREAST CANCER

Signs and symptoms. The only symptom of breast cancer is the finding of a lump in the breast. As already explained in Chapter 5, all women should examine their breasts regularly, and report any lumps they may find to their doctor. Even if you do discover a lump, there is a good chance that it is not cancerous, but if it is, think positively, and take advice on the most appropriate way to treat your particular lump.

Treatment. Breast cancer can be attacked on three fronts:

1. Surgical. Depending on the stage and position of your lump, your surgeon may decide to:

    a) remove the lump only;

    b) remove a segment of your breast;

    c) remove the whole breast. This can be a 'simple mastectomy', or a 'radical mastectomy' in which the tissue underlying the breast is also removed. This latter operation is not done so frequently these days, due to the advances in other, associated, forms of treatment. This treatment can be followed up by:

2. Radiotherapy. This involves a course of treatment by deep X-rays for four or five weeks. The actual period of each treatment is very short. Some people may have unpleasant side-effects such as nausea or extreme fatigue. If this happens to you, be gentle with yourself during this time. Do not try and 'keep going' at all costs. Rest up for a while and give your body as good a chance as possible to recuperate.

3. Hormone therapy. Whether or not this type of treatment is suitable for you will depend on the type of tumour that has grown

in your breast. New treatments are continually being evolved for the treatment of breast cancer, so be guided by your specialist. Remember that many women who have, or have had, breast cancer die of a completely unrelated disease. If you do have to submit to surgery of your breast, the Mastectomy Association offers valuable support and advice. The address is, The Mastectomy Association, 26 Harrison Street (off Gray's Inn Road), London WC1H 8JG, telephone 01-837 0908. This association works in close liaison with hospital departments and nurses in the care of women with cancer of the breast.

PROSTATIC CANCER
The prostate gland is an organ situated around the base of the bladder. In older men, benign enlargement of this gland is common. Due to the prostate gland's close proximity to the bladder, any enlargement will give problems with the passage of urine. Unfortunately, these symptoms are similar to those produced by a cancer of the prostate. So, any man over fifty who has:
1. difficulty in passing urine;
2. an interrupted, or slow, stream of urine;
3. signs of a urinary tract infection, namely, pain on passing urine and the need to pass urine frequently,
should contact his doctor. A simple rectal examination will tell the doctor, with a good deal of accuracy, whether the problems are due to a simple benign enlargement of the prostate or whether there is a possibility of cancer. Your general practitioner may well wish to refer you to a specialist who is skilled in this field of medicine.
Treatment. Hormone treatment is the treatment of choice in prostatic cancer. Female hormones effectively dampen down the secretion of the male hormone and this causes the cancer to regress. Sometimes the testes – the organs that produce the male hormone – are also removed, as is the prostate itself on occasion.

There are, of course, very many other sites in the body where cancer can develop – lung, bowel, brain, skin to mention just a few. Signs and symptoms of these will vary with the place where they are situated.

If you make sure to contact your doctor in any of the events listed on pages 108–9 (under 'When to contact the doctor' in Chapter 5) you will be sure to pick up the earliest sign of any problem. The earlier treatment is begun, the more likely are the chances of a complete cure.

There is a useful organisation, BACUP (British Association of Cancer United Patients), which provides excellent advice, sympathy and information for people who have cancer and their families. This organisation was started in 1985 by a woman doctor who herself was a cancer sufferer. Experienced cancer nurses are available to answer telephone queries on any aspect of cancer from 9.30 a.m. to 5.30 p.m., Mondays to Fridays. Leaflets on various aspects of the diseases are also available. Patients, friends, family, doctors or nurses are all welcome to call. The telephone number is 01-608 1661.

CATARACT

This is a condition affecting the lens of the eye as age increases. Instead of being completely transparent, the jelly-like substance of which the lens consists becomes cloudy and rays of light are not focused so clearly on the retina at the back of the eye.

Signs and symptoms.

1. Formation of cataracts is usually so gradual that sufferers are unable to say just when their vision first began to deteriorate. But in retrospect, they will be able to say that, for example, their vision is not as clear as it was a year ago.

2. It will become necessary to sit near a bright light to sew, read or do fine handwork of any kind.

Treatment. The optician to whom you go for regular checks of your vision will probably be the first person to be aware of a developing cataract. Because your vision is worsening, you will think that your glasses need changing, but it may be the changes in the lens of your eye that are causing the problem, and not the problem of accommodation to near objects that is the common complaint.

Cataracts develop slowly. In the early stages – and this may be years – extra magnification (by spectacles or a lens held in the hand) is all that is needed. A rearrangement of the lighting at home may also be of value. Have a reading lamp beside you in the evenings, and sit near a window to read during the daylight hours. You may never need any further treatment than this, but if you are restricted too much by your poor vision, an operation to remove the cataract is available. In this procedure, the clouded lens is removed. Without a lens, close vision is impossible, so an artificial lens must be provided. This can be done in one of three ways:

1. an artificial lens can be implanted at the time of the operation,
2. contact lenses can be fitted;
3. correcting spectacles can be provided.

The operation can be done under a local anaesthetic. This is not as fearsome as it sounds: you will be given a drug to relax you, and the local anaesthetic that is instilled into your eye will ensure that you feel no pain. But if you are extremely nervous about the prospect, the operation can be done under a general anaesthetic.

Cataracts conjure up in people's minds the fear of inevitable blindness. But this is far from the truth. Only operation can 'cure' the problems caused by the damaged lens, it is true. But with modern operating techniques results are excellent.

While on the subject of diminished vision, a word about the conditions that should lead you to contact your optician or your doctor as soon as possible:

1. If you *suddenly* become unable to see clearly.
2. If you suffer from double vision at any time.
3. If you have pain in your eye.
4. If you see 'haloes' of coloured light around lighted objects.
5. If you notice one isolated part of your visual field becoming dark.

None of these conditions is due to a developing cataract, but to other disease in the eye, and must be diagnosed and treated promptly.

DEMENTIA

Dementia is probably the condition that most of us fear as we approach the years beyond middle age. But do remember that there are many other conditions that cause a person to become confused and unable to think and behave logically, and many of these are eminently treatable. For example, conditions such as a failing heart, pneumonia or severe anaemia can give rise to similar changes. Thyroid disease, drug reactions or excessive alcohol intake are other long-term conditions which may also be at the root of the problem. Confusion due to the acute conditions such as pneumonia will, of course, be accompanied by other signs and symptoms and will also be of a comparatively sudden onset, while other conditions may manifest themselves only slowly. So medical advice must be sought to eliminate the other causes of unusual behaviour.

The most common cause of dementia seen today is known as Alzheimer's disease. The cause of this condition is not known, so no specific treatment, or preventive methods, are as yet available.
Signs and symptoms.

1. Loss of memory. This is far more extensive than the normal lapses which happen to all of us at times. Often the sufferer will be able to remember events that occurred in his or her childhood with greater clarity than what happened yesterday.

2. Emotions – manifested by excessive laughing or crying – become uncontrolled and often quite unlike the person's previous character.

3. The ability to plan ahead, even as far as preparing the next meal, will deteriorate until, in the worst stages, sufferers are unable to care for themselves.

(This may seem a gloomy list to some of us who always seem to be overlooking something on the shopping list or the birthday of an old friend. How many of us have forgotten to buy that so obviously necessary ingredient, and have laughed, rather hysterically, at the lapse? But take heart! These small lapses are quite unlike the persistent, wide-ranging problems associated with Alzheimer's disease.)

Treatment. No specific treatment is available, but there are a number of actions that can be taken to help the sufferer.

1. Most important of all is to ask your doctor, with perhaps a later referral to a specialist in such conditions, to check on all the other diseases which could lead to similar symptoms, many of which are treatable.

2. Check also on hearing and vision. If either of these faculties of awareness of the outside world is working below par, this can lead to confusion and withdrawal.

3. Encouragement to take a normal interest in day-to-day affairs, by watching television and reading newspapers or magazines can also help. Encourage also aids to memory such as shopping lists, birthday books etc. Remember, too, not to laugh at someone whose memory is less than perfect. Gently jog his or her memory with small clues – give time to think – praise success.

Dementia is a sad fact of life for sufferers and their families, especially when a comparatively young person is the victim. Alzheimer's disease – or 'pre-senile dementia', as used to be the common name – can affect people in their fifties, although it is more common in an older age-group.

Help can be obtained from your general practitioner, health visitor, social services or the Alzheimer Disease Society at Radcliffe Infirmary, Woodstock Road, Oxford OX2 6AG. This society will be able to give you advice on where to obtain extra help and support if you have a relative suffering from this condition.

DIABETES

Diabetes is caused by a failure of the pancreas to secrete adequate amounts of insulin, necessary for the proper control of sugar metabolism.

There are two forms of 'sugar' diabetes, **acute-onset diabetes**, which can occur at any time of life from two years of age onwards, and in which there is an almost complete lack of insulin, and **late-onset diabetes**, in which there is only a relative insulin deficiency. It is the latter type that may concern you as you reach retirement age. If you have had diabetes for a large part of your life you will know all about the problems, and be well able to cope with the care of your body by the time you come up to retirement.

Late-onset diabetes is sometimes considered to be a disease of western civilisation. (Diabetes was described as long ago as 1500 BC, so it is not a new disease in itself.) The high content of sugar and other carbohydrates in our diet, the tendency we have to overweight and our lack of exercise are all thought to be factors involved. Add to this the decreasing efficiency of the pancreas – along with all the other organs of our body – as we age, and you can see that the amount of insulin produced is unlikely to be sufficient to meet the needs of a high sugar intake. A family tendency to diabetes is also a factor, as about one quarter of diabetics have a relative with this condition.

Signs and symptoms are not as clear cut in late-onset diabetes as in the earlier acute-onset diabetes. These latter sufferers have an enormous thirst, pass large quantities of urine, lose weight rapidly and will quickly pass into a coma unless treatment is given. Diabetics in the older age group can exhibit these symptoms in a modified form, but often there may only be a generalised feeling of weariness and a craving for extra drinks and sweet food. Diagnosis is simply made by a urine test. If this proves positive – i.e. if sugar is being excreted in the urine – a blood test will clinch the diagnosis.

Treatment. In the acute diabetic state, regular injections of insulin to control the sugar metabolism are necessary. In a diabetic with a later onset, diet alone (reducing the intake of carbohydrates) may be all that is necessary. Treatment in tablet form may also be all that is necessary for some people. Your doctor must decide on what is best for you. Whatever treatment is necessary in your particular situation, it is important to keep regular daily checks to determine if any sugar is being excreted in your urine.

Diabetes can lead to other complications, especially if continuing and adequate treatment is not given.

1. The effect on the blood vessels of the body may show itself in a number of ways:

    a) an increased tendency to coronary artery disease;

    b) a high blood pressure;

    c) a condition known as 'intermittent claudication', in which the blood vessels of the legs become so narrowed as to cause pain when walking for any distance.

All these conditions are a direct result of the narrowing of the blood vessels.

2. Eye conditions, such as small haemorrhages in the retina causing blurred vision.

3. Damage to nerves supplying legs and arms can lead to muscular weakness and a diminution in sensation. Care must be taken to avoid falls.

4. Problems with healing if any injury occurs – particularly on the legs or feet. This is also associated with the poor blood supply so often associated with diabetes.

All these conditions can be reduced to a minimum by checking up a little more regularly on *your* 'body maintenance' by:

1. keeping firmly to the dietary regime prescribed for you;

2. checking your urine regularly every day;

3. attending your doctor, or the hospital, for regular check-ups;

4. visiting your optician regularly – especially if you have noticed any deterioration in your vision;

5. treating carefully any cuts or other injuries on your hands or feet: check with your doctor if they are not healing satisfactorily;

6. visiting the chiropodist regularly to keep feet in good trim: remember *never* to cut your own corns if you are diabetic.

The chances are high, if you follow these guidelines, that your diabetes will not have too much effect on the quality of your life.

DIVERTICULITIS

This condition of the large bowel is common in people over the age of fifty. As we mature, our lower bowel develops small 'blow-outs' where the wall of the bowel becomes thin and stretched – very much like a thinning tyre. The cause is again very much related to our refined diet: the condition is virtually unknown in countries where the diet contains a high proportion of roughage. The thinning and pouching of itself causes no symptoms, but when these pockets become blocked with waste material, infection, and maybe also ulceration, can supervene. This will then give rise to **symptoms** of:

1. Diarrhoea, which may also be associated with bouts of bleeding from the lower bowel.

2. Pain in the left lower part of the abdomen.

These symptoms will occur in bouts, often with many months between attacks.

Treatment.

1. The acute phase of this condition will need your doctor's help by way of antibiotics.

2. A diet high in fibre will do much to alleviate the symptoms, and also do much to prevent further episodes occurring.

It is important to check with your doctor if you have frequent symptoms. A cancer of the lower bowel must be excluded as a possible cause. A barium enema, and maybe a sigmoidoscopy, in which the lower bowel is looked into by a special instrument, may well be thought necessary to be sure that nothing more sinister is going on.

GALLSTONES

The gall-bladder is a small oval organ closely associated, both in function and situation, with the liver. It is tucked in under the ribs on the right side of the body. Its function is to store any excess bile, which is a necessary component in the satisfactory digestion of food. Owing to adverse chemical changes, 'stones' can form of varying chemical composition. This in itself will give rise to few symptoms, but when one or more of these stones, passing out through the bile-duct, gets stuck, problems can arise. As the stone tries to push its way through into the small intestine painful spasms occur. Although younger age groups can be affected, this is primarily a condition of middle age.

Signs and symptoms.

1. The sudden severe pain is felt in the top part of the abdomen, and may radiate up into the chest or to the tip of the right shoulder.

2. Vomiting and shock can result from the severity of the pain. At times this condition can be difficult to differentiate from an acute heart attack.

3. Jaundice – a yellow coloration of the skin – can also result. These symptoms are the typical picture of an acute attack of cholecystitis (inflammation of the gall-bladder). But many people with gallstones have long periods when they only suffer from vague feelings of discomfort in the upper part of their abdomen, ill-defined attacks of indigestion and maybe 'bilious' attacks where vomiting is a problem. These long-term discomforts may or may not be interspersed with acute attacks of pain.

Treatment.

1. To cure the condition the gall-bladder, together with its associated stones, must be removed surgically. This will mean a general anaesthetic and a stay in hospital of around eight to ten days. Before the operation special X-rays will need to be done, but following operation, the relief you will feel, when full recovery has occurred, will be immense. Some trials have been done on the dispersal of stones by ultra-sound.

166 · A *Guide to Positive Retirement*

2. If symptoms are not so severe as to be thought to warrant surgery (or while you are waiting for the operation), dietary treatment can do much to relieve symptoms. A diet as free from fat as possible must be your aim – no fried foods at all. Antacid medicines are also of value in controlling indigestion-like symptoms: buy the one which suits you best, but remember not to overdo the dosage. If you feel the need to take an antacid more than three times in any one day, you should make an appointment to see your doctor.

It always used to be taught that 'fair, fat females of forty' were the most likely sufferers from gallstones, but this is not necessarily so: men and older women can also suffer from this condition.

GLAUCOMA

After cataract formation, glaucoma is the commonest condition affecting the eyes of people in the retirement age group. Normally there is free drainage and circulation of the fluid in the eye: in glaucoma, part of this system becomes blocked leading to a build-up of pressure in the anterior part of the eye.

Signs and symptoms.

1. A dull, continuous pain in the eye, associated with watering of the eye and headache.

2. Vision becomes blurred and, as the disease progresses, peripheral vision is reduced so much that the sufferer is unable to see anyone – or anything – approaching from the side. (This can, of course, lead to accidents if traffic is involved.)

3. Nausea, and even actual vomiting, can occur.

4. Green or multi-coloured haloes around a light source such as a street lamp, is also a warning sign of glaucoma.

It is important to obtain treatment for glaucoma early. If this is not done, peripheral vision becomes more and more restricted until only 'tunnel' (i.e. straight ahead) vision remains and eventually, blindness can result. If you notice any of these symptoms, go to your doctor straight away.

Treatment is of two kinds, depending on the type of glaucoma.

1. Treatment with eye-drops, either alone or in association with tablets, will halt the condition in many cases.

2. Surgical treatment, in which a small piece of the iris (the coloured part of the eye) is removed. This allows adequate drainage to take place through the artificial channel that has been made.

GOUT

This is still a condition that gives rise to much mirth, conjuring up a picture of a red-nosed, irascible old gentleman with a heavily bandaged foot propped up on a stool and a glass of port in his hand. But it is not quite so amusing if you are the person affected – especially if you hate port.

Signs and symptoms. Gout is caused by a high level of uric acid in the blood. The crystals of this substance become deposited in some of the smaller joints of the body, giving rise to excruciating pain, especially when the joint is moved. The joints of the big toes are most frequently involved, but fingers, knees and elbows can also be involved. The attacks come in bouts, often with long periods of time between episodes. If the attacks are not adequately treated each time, permanent deformity in the joint can result. Damage can occur in the kidneys also – again due to the same high level of uric acid.

Treatment.

1. Rest of the affected joint which can be red, hot and very swollen during an acute attack.

2. Anti-inflammatory and pain-killing drugs, together with a specific drug.

3. Long-term treatment can involve:

    a) a regular low dose of the specific anti-gout drug;

    b) a diet low in protein;

    c) a reduction in wine drinking (especially fortified wines such as port).

Gout is rarely a serious disease, but it can result in a good deal of discomfort and disability – often without much sympathy from people who are not sufferers.

HEART ATTACK

Heart conditions of all kinds cause about half of all the deaths in western countries. The most common of these conditions is coronary thrombosis. Here one of the coronary arteries, the tiny blood vessels supplying the heart, becomes blocked. As a result, the part of the heart muscle supplied by that blood vessel dies and the normal, regular heart beat cannot be maintained. The reason why coronary arteries become blocked is that the lining of the walls of these (and other) arteries becomes invaded by fatty tissue. These deposits effectively narrow the 'bore' of these tiny arteries over the years. (Remember that the coronary arteries are no thicker than a piece of string.) So one more deposit of fatty tissue, or a clumping together of the blood cells, or a spasm of the artery can result in a heart attack.

The reason why westerners are so prone to coronary thrombosis is thought to be due largely to our lifestyle. Factors contributing are:

1. Overweight and lack of exercise. Much overweight could be eliminated if fats – particularly the saturated animal fats – were reduced in our diet. By more regular exercise, weight can be controlled as well as ensuring that the heart is in as good a condition as possible.

2. Cigarette smoking is known to have a specific effect on blood vessels.

3. Heredity also plays a part. The type of metabolism as well as physical characteristics are all inherited from our parents. If there is a high incidence of heart disease in the immediate family, there is more likelihood of similar problems arising.

4. High blood pressure has also been considered to be a factor in the onset of heart attacks, although the recent Medical Research Council trial into this aspect of circulatory disease did not prove

this conclusively. However, for other circulatory reasons (for example, strokes), high blood pressure must always be treated.

Coronary disease is no respecter of age or sex. Men in their twenties can suffer, although the highest incidence of the disease is in men in their fifties. Women are less likely to be affected in the earlier age-groups but the incidence increases with age.

Signs and symptoms. A coronary thrombosis will give rise to some or all of the following symptoms:

1. Sudden, severe pain in the *middle* of the chest. This pain is described as 'gripping' or 'vice-like'. The pain can also often be felt in the arms – the left arm in particular.

2. Breathlessness.

3. Feelings of giddiness and faintness.

Unconsciousness will supervene if the thrombus has affected one of the larger coronary vessels – and death can occur in minutes under these circumstances.

This is the most severe type of heart attack. More minor (but nevertheless worrying) attacks can occur with similar, but less severe, symptoms. As a general rule, if the sufferer has survived a heart attack for twelve hours, chances of recovery are good.

Angina pectoris, which literally means 'pain in the chest', is a condition with a similar background. Here the coronary arteries do not become blocked, but they become so narrowed, by either fatty deposits or spasm, that the heart is not receiving sufficient blood to be able to work at optimum efficiency.

The **symptoms** of this condition are:

1. Breathlessness on exertion of any kind.

2. Pain, again in the centre of the chest and maybe radiating up into the throat or to the arms.

To over-simplify, the subtle difference between angina and a heart attack is that angina occurs when the heart is overloaded, for example, during exercise, stress, emotion etc., while a coronary thrombosis occurs out of the blue. Angina may be a forerunner – or a warning sign – of a coronary thrombosis, so it must always be taken seriously and receive proper attention.

Treatment.

1. Coronary thrombosis. This is an emergency and medical aid must be obtained as soon as possible. Meanwhile:
- Loosen all tight clothing.
- Sit patient in the most comfortable position for him – usually semi-recumbent with the back against a chair or the wall.
- Reassure him.
- Keep him warm.
- If he stops breathing, apply mouth-to-mouth resuscitation if you are able.

These are all first aid measures until the doctor or ambulance arrives. A 999 call is the best way to obtain help if your own doctor is not immediately available. Specialised treatment and monitoring in an intensive care unit will be necessary for several days following a coronary thrombosis.

2. Angina.

a) Drugs to dilate the narrowed coronary arteries are the mainstay of treatment. Anyone who suffers from angina will have a supply of tablets ready to take if an attack occurs.

b) Coronary bypass operations are now becoming more common. A vein from some other part of the body replaces one of the narrowed coronary arteries.

c) Some people, whose hearts are not working efficiently, due to either angina or perhaps a previous attack of coronary thrombosis, will need extra medication in the form of diuretic drugs ('water tablets'). These drugs help to eliminate excess water from the body, which the failing heart is not able to do efficiently. Further drugs, such as those to strengthen the heart muscle or to correct arhythmias (irregular heart-beat), may also be necessary.

Much research has been done, and is still proceeding, into heart disease, this scourge of modern civilisation. The doctor has at his disposal a large armoury of drugs to treat heart problems. Cardiologists – specialists in heart disease – are to be found in every district general hospital. But *you* are the only person who can ensure that you stick to a healthy lifestyle, the best 'treatment' of all to counteract heart disease.

HIATUS HERNIA

Many people have a hiatus hernia, and probably know nothing about it. In this condition a small portion of the stomach is pushed up through the diaphragm into the chest cavity. (The diaphragm is the big sheet of muscle that separates the chest cavity from the abdominal cavity. The gullet, or oesophagus, pierces the diaphragm, and it is through this opening that the stomach passes when a hiatus hernia is present.)

As we get older all our muscles become slack, and this includes the diaphragm and its associated structures: the muscle is no longer strong enough to hold the stomach in the correct position. Overweight, with excess fat pushing against weakened muscles, can be a factor in the onset of a hiatus hernia.

Signs and symptoms.

1. Feelings of discomfort in the upper part of the abdomen – especially after a large meal.

2. 'Heartburn' – that unpleasant sore feeling, again in the upper part of the abdomen.

3. Regurgitation of acid fluid into the mouth.

All these symptoms are caused by a low-grade inflammation in the part of the stomach that is misplaced.

Treatment.

1. Small, frequent meals rather than fewer large ones.

2. Do not eat late at night.

3. Sleep with a number of pillows.

4. Antacids – from your doctor or the chemist.

5. Lose weight, if this is a factor.

6. Operation to tighten up the opening in the diaphragm. This is rarely necessary, as the simpler measures usually alleviate the symptoms.

*　　　*　　　*

A common condition. Consult your doctor if you think that your symptoms may be due to a hiatus hernia.

OSTEOPOROSIS

Osteoporosis is not in itself a disease, rather a condition that can lead to problems in middle age, especially in women. Leading up to and during the menopause there is a weakening of the bone structure of the body. Calcium in particular is lost from the bones due to hormonal changes, causing softening and brittleness of the bones so that fractures become relatively more common after even a simple fall. Osteoporosis is also the reason why many elderly people – both men and women – lose height. The vertebrae making up the spine become thinned and the intervertebral discs flattened, resulting in the typical loss of height, often together with a hunched back.

There is no specific treatment guaranteed to prevent osteoporosis, but there are a few steps that can be taken to reduce problems to a minimum.

1. Calcium and vitamin D supplements can be taken, especially by women around the time of the menopause. (Vitamin D is necessary for the proper absorption of calcium.) Calcium is best taken in a dissolvable form. Such products can be obtained from any chemist or on prescription from your doctor if he thinks this form of treatment would benefit you.

2. Adequate exercise will stimulate the replacement of bone following the natural 'wear and tear' process.

3. A diet rich in calcium and vitamin D will also help – dairy products and oily fish in particular.

4. If you are a woman at the menopause, your doctor may consider hormone replacement therapy to be suitable for you. This will effectively counteract the tendency to lose calcium.

5. Avoid injury as far as you are able. A trip over a step, saving yourself with your hands, is more likely to result in a fractured wrist than a similar accident would have done in your younger days.

6. There have been recent reports about a substance – calcitonin – that can be either injected or given as a nasal spray which will significantly help with the problems of osteoporosis.

Again – a common condition as we mature, but one which you can do something about with a little forethought, and maybe some small changes in your lifestyle.

PARKINSON'S DISEASE

This condition is due to chemical changes in the brain associated with ageing. About one in a hundred people over the age of sixty will be affected by Parkinson's disease. The degree of severity will vary very much from person to person, and it will certainly not be an incapacitating illness for all these people.

Signs and symptoms.

1. A tremor, particularly noticeable in the hands, and at its worst when the muscles are relaxed. Any movement temporarily inhibits the tremor, but this will return again once relaxation in a different position occurs.

2. Stiffness of movement. This is especially noticeable in the muscles of the face in a person with a severe degree of disability. The face will appear expressionless and immobile. This stiffness will obviously have an effect on movement, especially walking.

3. Slowness of movement, due to the combination of tremor and stiffness.

4. The above symptoms can have marked effects on speaking, walking and fine movements such as writing.

5. An associated depressive illness can often result from this condition, and this is understandable. But with a positive outlook and treatment Parkinson's disease need not make life completely miserable.

Treatment.

1. Certain drugs – from either your own doctor or a specialist in this condition – will do much to alleviate the symptoms.

2. Physiotherapy is vitally important to help with walking and other movements.

3. The advice of a speech therapist is also very valuable in helping to make full use of face and tongue muscles used in speech.

4. Occupational therapy can assist in the control of fine movements, and also has the benefit of introducing the sufferer into a whole new range of interests.

Parkinson's disease need not be as incapacitating as it may appear at first sight, but it will require hard work and a positive attitude on the part of the sufferer to counteract the worst effects. The Parkinson's Disease Society, 36 Portland Place, London W1N 3DG has useful literature available, and will also be able to put you in touch with your nearest local branch of the society.

SHINGLES

This condition, although it can affect any age group, is relatively common in late middle age. And most unpleasant and long-lasting can it be at this time of life.

Shingles is a virus infection of specific nerve roots. Any part of the body can be affected, although the nerve endings around the ribs are among the commoner sites. Ulceration of the cornea of the eye is an especially nasty complication of an attack of shingles around the head.

It used to be thought that shingles followed contact with someone (usually a child) who was suffering from chickenpox. Today's thinking is more inclined to the view that the virus (which is very similar to the virus of chickenpox) has lain dormant in the body for a number of years. At a time when the body is at a low ebb for some reason, this virus becomes active.

Signs and symptoms.

1. Initially there is acute pain in the area of the body that is affected. For example, a band around one side of the chest

following the line of one or two of the intercostal nerves, on one side of the face, or even down the inside of a leg.

2. After about a week, the typical blistery rash (again very like that of chickenpox) appears. After a few days this rash will crust over and it will take fourteen days or so to disappear.

3. In older people particularly, pain following the clearing of the condition can, unfortunately, be severe and long-lasting.

4. Many older sufferers feel very unwell during the acute stages of the infection – seemingly out of all proportion to the visible rash. Not a feeling to be dismissed as neurotic. Be gentle with yourself at this time. It *will* pass, however unlikely this may seem to you at the time.

Treatment.

1. Aspirin, paracetamol or a more powerful painkiller from your doctor during the acute stages of the disease will be necessary. (You may also need the painkillers for a while after the rash has disappeared if the pain is still persistent. You are not imagining it – it really does happen.)

2. Calamine lotion on the rash can help, as can a little sodium bicarbonate in the bath water. Recently a cream and tablets have become available which, if used early enough in the disease, can cut down both the pain and the length of time the rash is a problem, but treatment must be begun early.

3. Plenty of rest and a good nourishing diet if you are feeling unwell with the infection.

4. Remember to drink plenty of fluids also.

5. If the infection has affected your eye, it is a good idea to have your vision checked by an ophthalmologist to be sure that no permanent damage has been done.

Shingles can be an unpleasant disease – not dangerous, but nevertheless one which can make you feel very unwell for a month or two.

STROKE

Strokes of one kind or another are the third commonest cause of death in the western world, after heart disease and cancer. A stroke is a condition affecting the blood vessels in the brain. The severity of the condition can vary very markedly. The most minor forms of stroke can be a mere drooping of an eyelid or a feeling of weakness in one part of the body for a few hours, for example. These symptoms can clear quite quickly – within a day or two. This type of minor stroke occurs when a small blood vessel only is involved, and other adjacent vessels are able to take over the blood supply of the part that has been affected. At the other end of the scale is the devastating sudden stroke which is either immediately fatal or leaves the sufferer paralysed and maybe without speech. And obviously there are ranges of severity in between these two extremes.

Basically there are two forms of stroke – those due to a **cerebral haemorrhage**, in which a blood vessel in the brain ruptures, causing bleeding into the surrounding area and damage to the brain tissue, and those due to a **cerebral thrombosis**, in which a blood vessel becomes blocked as in a coronary thrombosis. The onset of these two conditions is quite different.

Possible causative factors.

1. A high blood pressure is an important factor in the onset of a stroke. So in the early retirement years it is important to have your blood pressure checked regularly by your doctor. He will advise, and institute treatment, if the level is too high over several readings.

2. The factors that have a bearing on the onset of a coronary thrombosis also apply to strokes – especially to the cerebral thrombosis type. The blood vessels in the brain can become narrowed by fatty deposits in the same way as the coronary arteries.

Signs and symptoms.

1. Cerebral haemorrhage
   a) The onset is sudden.

b) A severe headache, maybe associated with vomiting, may occur before the sufferer becomes unconscious.

c) Unconsciousness may result without the preceding symptoms of headache and vomiting.

d) It is often obvious that one side of the body is paralysed in a severe stroke.

2. Cerebral thrombosis

a) This is an altogether slower onset illness.

b) The first sign may be a weakness in one part of the body – a hand or a leg – which is manifested by the person's dropping something or falling down.

c) Loss of consciousness does not usually occur immediately, but may occur over the following hours or days if the thrombus extends.

Treatment will vary according to the severity and type of stroke. Immediate first aid care and contact with your own doctor should be your first concern.

Following direct treatment, physiotherapy to help restore the function that remains after healing has occurred, in the severe cases where paralysis has resulted. Speech therapy may also be necessary to help with speech problems if the area of the brain that is concerned with speech has been affected.

An enormous amount of help is available from many sources, both statutory and voluntary, for people who have suffered a stroke. If this happens to a relative of yours do make enquiries and 'get plugged into' all the sources that are available locally. The Chest, Heart and Stroke Association, Tavistock House North, Tavistock Square, London WC1L 9JE will provide you with useful information about what is available in your locality.

THYROID DISEASE

Disease of the thyroid gland is a not uncommon, and possibly under-diagnosed, problem, particularly in middle-aged women. The secretions of this gland, which is situated in the neck, are

vitally important for many aspects of daily living. Various problems – at all times of life – can occur in this gland, giving rise to
wide-ranging and complex problems, but in middle age the most
common disorder is an under-functioning of the gland – a condition known as 'myxoedema' or 'hypothyroidism'.

Signs and symptoms.

1. The onset of the symptoms can be so gradual as to pass
unnoticed for many months. In fact, the general slowing down
associated with myxoedema is often thought to be due to the
normal ageing process. (Yet one more reason to avoid saying, 'It's
my age' – it may not be.)

2. Lethargy, and a general lack of 'get up and go' are common
symptoms. If this is happening to someone you know who previously was full of energy and activity, it is always wise to get
advice.

3. A puffy face with a dry skin and a typical swelling around the
eyes.

4. The voice can be lowered about an octave, and always seems
to be croaky.

5. Sufferers will feel the cold intensely, and may also suffer
from constipation.

In fact the picture is one of a general slowing down of all bodily
functions. A blood test will clinch the diagnosis. Unpleasant for
the sufferer, and irritating for those around her – also quite
unnecessary, as treatment is simple once the correct diagnosis has
been made.

Treatment. Hormone replacement therapy – one or two small
tablets daily is usual – is all that is needed to restore the sufferer to
normal health. The hormone will have to be taken for life, but this
is a small price to pay for feeling well again.

VARICOSE VEINS

Varicose veins are not a condition confined to the middle-aged
group, but older people, especially women who have borne

children, are more likely to be afflicted. Varicose veins are caused by a failure of the tiny valves in the superficial veins of the legs. This allows the blood to pool in these dilated veins and so produce the blueish, knotted swellings so commonly seen on middle-aged legs. Several factors have a bearing on the occurrence of varicose veins:

1. Heredity. There is almost always a strong family history of varicose veins.

2. Race. Some races, such as African peoples, rarely suffer from varicose veins. The Caucasian races seem particularly prone to the condition.

3. Overweight, causing back-pressure on the veins of the legs.

4. Pregnancy, in the same way as overweight, causes back-pressure on the veins of the legs. This may be the time of life at which varicose veins start – improvement is usual after the birth, but a worsening may well occur again in middle age.

Signs and symptoms.

1. Raised, knotted veins, usually on the calves of the legs.

2. Maybe aching legs after standing for any length of time.

3. Maybe varicose pigmentation below the site of the varicose vein.

4. Maybe varicose ulceration if adequate treatment is not given.

5. Can be haemorrhage from a vein if knocked accidentally.

Treatment.

1. Support stockings. These must be of a quality strong enough to fully support the leg if wearing them is to be of any value. Your doctor can prescribe them for you.

2. Injection treatment, where a sclerosing (hardening) fluid is injected into the varicose vein. Scarring is produced after several weeks, and this effectively blocks off the affected vein. Its work is taken over by an adjacent, healthy vein.

3. Operation, the most usual surgical treatment today is the 'tie-off' operation, where the varicosed vein is tied off as it perforates a tough, fibrous sheath which separates it from the

deeper vessels of the leg. Again, its function is taken over by other nearby veins. Support bandaging and regular exercise (three miles a day) are important parts of follow-on treatment after both injection and operative treatments.

Quite apart from the cosmetic effect, it is as well to get advice about your varicose veins if they cause you trouble or are unsightly. Effective treatment will prevent the complications of pigmentation and – most unpleasant of all – ulceration. Varicose ulceration is notoriously difficult to heal, so avoiding its onset is a sensible precaution.

Useful addresses

Age Concern
60 Pitcairn Road, Mitcham, Surrey CR4 3LL

'Choice' magazine
Bedford Chambers, 12 Bedford Row, London WC2E 8HA

Citizens Advice Bureau
Local branches to be found in telephone book

Cruse
29 Sheen Road, Richmond, Surrey TW9 1UR

Dept. of Health & Social Security (for leaflets)
Alexander Fleming House, Newington Causeway, Elephant and Castle,
London SE1 6BY

Help the Aged
16–18 St James's Walk, London EC1R 0BE

National Council for Carers & their Elderly Dependants
29 Chilworth Mews, London W2 3RG

National Council for Voluntary Organisations
26 Bedford Square, London WC1B 3HU

Pre-Retirement Association
19 Undine Street, London SW17 8PP

Social Security Offices
In local telephone book under 'Health & Social Security'

HEALTH

Arthritis Care
6 Grosvenor Crescent, London SW1X 7ER

British Association for Cancer United Patients (BACUP)
121–123 Charterhouse Street, London EC1M 6AA
telephone: 01-608 1661

British Diabetic Association
10 Queen Anne Street, London W1M 0BD

The Chest, Heart & Stroke Association
Tavistock House North, Tavistock Square, London WC1L 9JE

Mastectomy Association
26 Harrison Street, London WC1H 8JG
Parkinson's Disease Society
36 Portland Place, London W1N 3DG

HOLIDAYS

Saga Holidays
Saga Buildings, Middelburg Square, Folkestone, Kent CT20 1AZ
(See also p. 142)

WORK

REACH
89 Southwark Street, London SE1 0HD
Small Firms Service
Telephone Freefone 2444
Success after Sixty
40–41 Old Bond Street, London W1X 3AF

Index